APIs with Django

Design, Develop, and Deploy High-Performance REST APIs Using Python and DRF

Jose Gobert

Copyright Page

Table of Contents

Preface 6

Chapter 1: APIs and Django REST Framework 8

What Are APIs 8

REST and GraphQL: Choosing the Right Tool 12

Overview of Django and Django REST Framework 16

Setting Up Your Development Environment 20

Creating Your First API Project 23

Chapter 2: Designing RESTful APIs 28

Core Principles of REST 28

Resource Modeling and Endpoint Planning 33

URI Conventions, HTTP Methods, and Status Codes 38

API Versioning Strategies 43

Documenting Design with OpenAPI and Swagger 48

Chapter 3: Building Your Data Layer with Django Models 53

Modeling Real-World Data with Django ORM 53

Managing Relationships and Constraints 57

Writing Clean, Maintainable Models 62

Initial Migrations and Data Seeding 66

Integrating Model Logic into API Design 70

Chapter 4: Serializers and Views in Depth 77

Serializers and Model Serializers 77

Validation Strategies and Custom Serializer Fields 82

APIViews, Generic Views, and ViewSets 87

Building Reusable View Logic with Mixins 92

Customizing View Behavior and Responses 97

Chapter 5: Authentication, Permissions, and Security 103

Django's Built-In User Model and Auth System 103

Token Authentication and JWT Integration 108

Writing Custom Permissions and Access Rules 114

Role-Based Access Control (RBAC) 119

Rate Limiting, Throttling, and Securing Sensitive Endpoints 124

Chapter 6: Querying, Filtering, and Pagination 131

Filtering with Django Filter Backend 131

Searching and Ordering API Results 137

Nested Resources and Lookup Fields 142

Pagination Schemes and Custom Pagination Classes...................147

Optimizing Database Queries for Performance 153

Chapter 7: Testing and Debugging Your API 159

Introduction to API Testing Principles 159

Unit and Integration Testing with DRF and pytest 163

Test Coverage, Fixtures, and Factories 169

Mocking External Dependencies..175

Debugging API Issues and Using DRF's Browsable Interface 180

Chapter 8: Building a Real-World API Project........................... 186

Project Brief: Designing a Real Application (Task Manager) 186

Domain Modeling and Architecture.................................... 190

Building Core Features and Workflows 195

Securing, Validating, and Testing the Project.............................200

Exposing the API for Frontend Consumption 206

Chapter 9: Preparing for Production 213

Production Settings and Environment Variables 213

Static Files, Media, and File Uploads 218

Logging, Error Handling, and Monitoring............................ 223

Dockerizing Your Django API 229

Deployment with Gunicorn, Nginx, and PostgreSQL.................... 234

Chapter 10: Documentation, CI/CD, and Beyond 241

Auto-Generating API Docs with Swagger and ReDoc 241

API Versioning and Change Management 246

Creating a CI/CD Pipeline with GitHub Actions 252

Scaling, Caching, and Performance Tuning 256

Next Steps: Async APIs, Celery, and Microservices...................... 262

Conclusion 268

Preface

In the ever-evolving landscape of web development, APIs are the backbone of modern applications. Whether it's powering a mobile app, integrating with third-party services, or building the backend for a dynamic single-page application, APIs enable the seamless exchange of data and functionality between systems. In a world that increasingly demands scalability, interoperability, and performance, mastering API development isn't just optional—it's essential.

This book was born from years of working with Django and Django REST Framework (DRF) in real-world projects—ranging from rapid prototypes to enterprise-scale systems. Along the way, I've seen many developers struggle not just with learning the tools, but with applying them effectively to create clean, well-architected, secure APIs that can stand the test of time. My goal in writing this book is to take you beyond the basics and into the realm of professional-grade API development with Django.

Why Django and DRF?

Python remains one of the most accessible and productive languages for web development, and Django has long been praised for its maturity, clarity, and batteries-included approach. Django REST Framework extends this philosophy into the API space, offering an incredibly powerful and flexible toolkit for building robust RESTful services. Whether you're a Python developer stepping into backend APIs for the first time or a seasoned engineer looking to sharpen your skills, this combination gives you the speed of development without sacrificing scalability or structure.

What You'll Learn

This book is more than just a how-to guide. It's a journey—from setting up your environment and building your first serializer to designing scalable APIs, securing endpoints, optimizing performance, writing tests, deploying to production, and even building an end-to-end real-world project. You won't just learn how to use DRF—you'll understand why certain design decisions matter, what trade-offs you face in practice, and how to think like an API architect, not just an implementer.

Each chapter is designed to build progressively, offering in-depth explanations, complete working examples, and best practices gleaned from real production systems. You'll encounter everything from token-based authentication and role-based access control to filtering, pagination, Docker deployment, and CI/CD pipelines.

Who This Book Is For

This book is written for developers who already have a basic understanding of Python and Django. You don't need to be an expert, but you should be comfortable working with models, views, and templates. If you've ever built a Django app and now want to expose its functionality as a REST API—or build a new one from scratch—this book is for you.

If you're coming from a different framework or language and want to learn Django and DRF from the perspective of building APIs, this book will also serve you well. It's especially suited for full-stack developers, backend engineers, and technical leads who want a deeper understanding of building maintainable, scalable, and production-ready APIs.

How to Use This Book

You can read this book cover to cover, or jump into chapters as needed. If you're just starting out, I recommend following the sequence as each chapter builds on the last. If you're already experienced and need guidance on something specific—like JWT authentication, testing, or deployment—you can head directly to that chapter.

At the end of the book, we'll put everything into practice by building and deploying a complete real-world project that encapsulates all the techniques and best practices you've learned.

Technology changes. APIs evolve. Frameworks get updated. But the core principles of good software design, clean architecture, secure data handling, and maintainable code endure. My hope is that this book not only helps you master Django and DRF for today—but equips you with the mindset and confidence to adapt and grow in the ever-changing tech landscape.

Thank you for joining me on this journey. Let's build something great—one endpoint at a time.

Chapter 1: APIs and Django REST Framework

What Are APIs

An API—short for **Application Programming Interface**—is a structured way for software applications to communicate with each other. Think of it like a common language, with agreed-upon rules and behavior. When one piece of software wants to retrieve or send data to another, it uses an API to make that request and receive a structured response.

The term "interface" is important here. In everyday language, an interface is what allows you to interact with something. A car has a steering wheel, pedals, and buttons—that's your interface to the vehicle. In software, the interface is often invisible to the user, but essential for machines to work together. A frontend application, such as a React-based admin panel, doesn't fetch data directly from the database. Instead, it sends a request to the backend through an API. The backend receives that request, processes it, and sends back a response—usually in a structured format like JSON.

Let's take a practical example. Suppose you're building an e-commerce platform. Your users want to view products, add items to their cart, and place orders. Your frontend application doesn't know anything about the database or how data is stored. What it does know is that when it sends an HTTP GET request to `/api/products/`, it expects to receive a list of available products. This contract between the client and the server is enforced and defined by the API.

Here's what that might look like in a real-world scenario using Django REST Framework.

First, you'd define your data model. Let's say we're working with a `Product` model:

```
from django.db import models

class Product(models.Model):
    name = models.CharField(max_length=255)
```

```python
    description = models.TextField()
    price = models.DecimalField(max_digits=10,
decimal_places=2)
    in_stock = models.BooleanField(default=True)

    def __str__(self):
        return self.name
```

Then you'd create a serializer to convert this model into JSON:

```python
from rest_framework import serializers
from .models import Product

class
ProductSerializer(serializers.ModelSerializer):
    class Meta:
        model = Product
        fields = '__all__'
```

Now you can expose it via an API endpoint:

```python
from rest_framework import viewsets
from .models import Product
from .serializers import ProductSerializer

class ProductViewSet(viewsets.ModelViewSet):
    queryset = Product.objects.all()
    serializer_class = ProductSerializer
```

Then wire it into your URLs:

```python
from django.urls import path, include
from rest_framework.routers import DefaultRouter
from .views import ProductViewSet

router = DefaultRouter()
router.register(r'products', ProductViewSet)

urlpatterns = [
    path('api/', include(router.urls)),
]
```

Once this is set up, a GET request to /api/products/ might return:

```json
[
  {
    "id": 1,
    "name": "Wireless Mouse",
    "description": "Ergonomic wireless mouse with 2.4GHz connectivity.",
    "price": "29.99",
    "in_stock": true
  },
  {
    "id": 2,
    "name": "Mechanical Keyboard",
    "description": "Compact mechanical keyboard with blue switches.",
    "price": "74.50",
    "in_stock": false
  }
]
```

This response can now be consumed by any frontend—React, Vue, mobile app, or even another backend service. None of them need to know anything about your database schema or your internal logic. They only need to know how to make requests to your API and what kind of responses to expect.

This is the power of APIs. They **decouple** systems, allowing independent development, testing, and deployment of services. Your frontend team can work with mock API responses long before the backend is complete. Your mobile app can reuse the same API as your web frontend. If you later migrate from PostgreSQL to another data store, your API contract can remain unchanged—and your clients won't even notice.

This decoupling isn't just about convenience; it's foundational to modern software architecture. If you're building a monolithic application today, APIs still help you structure your code clearly and make parts of it reusable. If you're working in a microservices environment, APIs are mandatory—they're how services communicate in a distributed system. Even in serverless setups, functions are typically exposed via APIs.

Consider a real-world integration. Let's say you want to send SMS notifications to users when their order status changes. You don't build an SMS delivery system from scratch—you use a third-party API like Twilio's. You authenticate with their service, send them a POST request with the message content and recipient number, and they handle the rest. You pay only for what you use, and you don't have to worry about carrier routing, message formatting, or global delivery regulations.

Here's what using Twilio's API might look like in Python:

```python
from twilio.rest import Client

client = Client("ACCOUNT_SID", "AUTH_TOKEN")

message = client.messages.create(
    body="Your order has been shipped!",
    from_="+1234567890",
    to="+1987654321"
)
```

This code is a reminder that APIs are not just about exposing your own data—they're also about tapping into powerful external services that expand what your applications can do.

In building APIs yourself, you're stepping into the critical infrastructure layer of your software. You're designing how data moves, how clients interact with your application, and how systems coordinate. A well-designed API feels intuitive and predictable. A poorly designed one leads to bugs, misunderstandings, and painful integrations.

To build APIs well, you need to think about data structure, consistency, performance, and security. You also need to think about versioning, error messages, and how your API might evolve over time. These are not optional concerns—they're part of the job. You're not just giving access to data; you're creating a contract that others will depend on.

That's what makes APIs so important. They are the public surface area of your backend. They're how your application talks to the world.

And that's why this book exists. By the time you reach the final chapter, you won't just know how to expose data from a Django app. You'll know how to **design, build, secure, test, document**, and **deploy** professional APIs that can be confidently used in production environments.

REST and GraphQL: Choosing the Right Tool

When you start building APIs, one of the decisions you'll face sooner or later is how to expose your data. The two most prominent options today are REST and GraphQL. Each offers a different philosophy, different trade-offs, and different expectations from the client and server. And the decision between them isn't always about which one is better. It's about choosing the tool that best fits the type of system you're building, the team you're working with, and the clients consuming your API.

REST has been around for a long time. It's a well-established architecture for creating web services using the principles of HTTP. The idea is simple: your system is made up of **resources**—things like users, products, orders—and you interact with them using **standard HTTP methods**. So, if you want to retrieve a product with ID 42, you make a GET request to `/products/42/`. If you want to update it, you make a PUT or PATCH request to the same URL. This pattern is consistent, predictable, and widely supported.

Let's take a practical example. Say you have a User model and you want to retrieve a user's profile information. With a REST API using Django REST Framework, your endpoint might look like this:

```
# models.py
from django.db import models

class UserProfile(models.Model):
    username = models.CharField(max_length=100)
    email = models.EmailField()
    bio = models.TextField(blank=True)

    def __str__(self):
        return self.username
# serializers.py
from rest_framework import serializers
from .models import UserProfile

class
UserProfileSerializer(serializers.ModelSerializer):
    class Meta:
        model = UserProfile
        fields = '__all__'
```

```
# views.py
from rest_framework import viewsets
from .models import UserProfile
from .serializers import UserProfileSerializer

class UserProfileViewSet(viewsets.ModelViewSet):
    queryset = UserProfile.objects.all()
    serializer_class = UserProfileSerializer
# urls.py
from rest_framework.routers import DefaultRouter
from .views import UserProfileViewSet

router = DefaultRouter()
router.register(r'profiles', UserProfileViewSet)

urlpatterns = [
    path('api/', include(router.urls)),
]
```

Now, your frontend can send a simple GET request to /api/profiles/1/ and receive all the data about that user in a single response. This is classic REST: resource-oriented, method-driven, and shaped around the HTTP protocol.

Now consider a different situation. Suppose you want to display a user's profile along with the list of posts they've written, and maybe also show the number of comments on each post. In REST, this can be challenging because you may need to make multiple requests: one for the user, one for the posts, and possibly additional ones for the comment counts.

This is where GraphQL starts to look attractive. Instead of multiple endpoints with fixed data shapes, GraphQL lets the client send a **single query** specifying exactly what fields it needs. This gives clients more control and can reduce the number of requests.

Here's what a GraphQL query might look like to achieve that:

```
query {
  user(id: 1) {
    username
    email
    posts {
      title
```

```
        commentCount
      }
    }
}
```

The server receives this query, processes it, and returns exactly the requested data—no more, no less. This flexibility is incredibly powerful, especially for applications with complex data needs, such as mobile apps with limited bandwidth or rich frontends that need to render deeply nested data structures.

So how does this actually work in code? Let's look at how you might implement that using Graphene, a popular GraphQL library for Django:

```python
# models.py
class Post(models.Model):
    user = models.ForeignKey(UserProfile,
on_delete=models.CASCADE, related_name='posts')
    title = models.CharField(max_length=255)

    @property
    def comment_count(self):
        return self.comments.count()
# schema.py
import graphene
from graphene_django import DjangoObjectType
from .models import UserProfile, Post

class PostType(DjangoObjectType):
    comment_count = graphene.Int()

    class Meta:
        model = Post
        fields = ('id', 'title', 'comment_count')

    def resolve_comment_count(self, info):
        return self.comment_count

class UserType(DjangoObjectType):
    class Meta:
        model = UserProfile
        fields = ('id', 'username', 'email',
'posts')
```

```
class Query(graphene.ObjectType):
    user = graphene.Field(UserType,
id=graphene.Int())

    def resolve_user(self, info, id):
        return UserProfile.objects.get(pk=id)

schema = graphene.Schema(query=Query)
```

With this setup, a single request gives the client complete control over what data to retrieve. No need for multiple round-trips. The client is in charge of shaping the response.

That's the core difference between REST and GraphQL. REST gives you a set of fixed endpoints with predictable behavior. GraphQL gives clients the power to request whatever they want, however deeply nested, from a single endpoint.

But with that power comes complexity. GraphQL servers are harder to cache, because every request can ask for different fields. You can't easily use standard HTTP caching strategies the way you can with REST. Also, your backend logic becomes more dynamic, which can make debugging and performance optimization more challenging. You may need to write custom resolvers for deeply nested fields or optimize your database queries to prevent the infamous "N+1" query problem.

There's also the matter of tooling. REST APIs have mature support in browsers, testing tools like Postman, documentation generators like Swagger/OpenAPI, and developer platforms. With Django REST Framework, for example, you get a browsable API out of the box that's great for testing and prototyping. GraphQL tools are improving, but they don't always integrate as smoothly in the Django ecosystem, especially if your team is already experienced with REST.

In practical terms, if you're building a standard web application or mobile backend where the data requirements are well understood and mostly stable, REST is often a simpler and more maintainable choice. It works beautifully with Django and DRF, and it scales well both in terms of performance and team structure.

On the other hand, if you're building a highly interactive frontend with a lot of nested data relationships, or if you want to give third-party developers precise control over the data they consume, GraphQL offers a lot of advantages—if you're willing to invest in its learning curve and infrastructure.

Both approaches are valid. Both are powerful. The right tool depends on the shape of your data, the needs of your clients, and the complexity you're prepared to manage. What matters most is understanding their trade-offs clearly so that you're not just choosing based on hype or habit, but making a decision that fits the architecture of your system and the realities of your team.

In this book, our focus is REST, and for good reason. Django REST Framework gives us a powerful set of tools to build professional-grade REST APIs quickly and safely. Once you've mastered it, you'll not only be able to build and maintain APIs effectively, but you'll also be better prepared to evaluate when and how to adopt alternatives like GraphQL in the future—if the need arises.

Overview of Django and Django REST Framework

Before we begin building our API, it's essential that we understand the two core tools we'll be working with throughout this book: **Django** and **Django REST Framework** (commonly referred to as DRF). These two frameworks are not just popular—they're practical, production-ready, and deeply capable. They've been tested at scale in thousands of real-world applications. But more importantly for you, they offer a clear and maintainable path to building high-performance APIs.

Let's start with Django. If you've already worked with it, this will reinforce what you know. If you're new, you'll see why Django continues to be a top choice for developers building web applications and services in Python.

Django is what's known as a **high-level Python web framework**. That simply means it's built to let you get from idea to working application as fast as possible, without sacrificing code quality or long-term maintainability. When Django says "batteries included," it truly means it. Out of the box, Django provides everything you need to build a secure, feature-rich backend: a powerful ORM (Object-Relational Mapper), routing, middleware, session handling, a user authentication system, a built-in admin interface, and a robust migration framework.

What makes Django different is how it encourages **clean design and convention**. It's not a blank canvas. It gives you strong opinions about project structure, naming, and flow—but it also stays flexible when you need it to. The framework is built around the Model-Template-View (MTV) pattern, which is Django's version of MVC. In this model, the data layer (models), the business logic and request handling (views), and the presentation layer (templates) are clearly separated.

But here's the thing: Django was originally designed for **web pages**, not APIs. That means if you use it by itself and want to build a JSON API, you'll spend a lot of time manually serializing data, handling HTTP verbs like PUT and DELETE yourself, and managing repetitive boilerplate code. This is where Django REST Framework steps in—and it changes the game completely.

Django REST Framework builds on top of Django and provides all the tools you need to create a fully-featured RESTful API. It integrates seamlessly with Django's models, views, and routing system, but it adds an abstraction layer specifically tailored for API development. This includes serialization tools for converting your models to and from JSON, class-based views designed for REST endpoints, robust authentication and permission handling, and even auto-generated documentation.

Let's make this real with a basic but complete example. We'll create a simple note-taking API using Django and DRF, just to see the pieces come together.

Start by defining a model. Open your models.py in a Django app called core and write:

```
from django.db import models

class Note(models.Model):
    title = models.CharField(max_length=255)
    content = models.TextField()
    created_at =
models.DateTimeField(auto_now_add=True)
```

```
def __str__(self):
    return self.title
```

This defines a model called `Note` with three fields. You can already interact with this model through Django's ORM, but now we want to expose it via an API.

The first step in DRF is to create a **serializer**. A serializer translates your model instance into JSON format and back again. It handles validation, data structure, and conversion logic.

In a new file `serializers.py`, add:

```
from rest_framework import serializers
from .models import Note

class NoteSerializer(serializers.ModelSerializer):
    class Meta:
        model = Note
        fields = '__all__'
```

With this, DRF knows how to convert `Note` instances into JSON and validate incoming JSON into proper model instances.

Next, you create a view. DRF provides several class-based views, and one of the most powerful is `ModelViewSet`. It automatically provides list, retrieve, create, update, and delete actions for a model. In `views.py`:

```
from rest_framework import viewsets
from .models import Note
from .serializers import NoteSerializer

class NoteViewSet(viewsets.ModelViewSet):
    queryset = Note.objects.all()
    serializer_class = NoteSerializer
```

The `NoteViewSet` tells DRF how to retrieve and serialize your notes.

Finally, you wire it up using DRF's router system. In your `urls.py`:

```
from django.urls import path, include
from rest_framework.routers import DefaultRouter
```

```
from core.views import NoteViewSet

router = DefaultRouter()
router.register(r'notes', NoteViewSet)

urlpatterns = [
    path('api/', include(router.urls)),
]
```

This automatically generates routes like:

GET `/api/notes/` — list all notes

POST `/api/notes/` — create a new note

GET `/api/notes/1/` — retrieve note with ID 1

PUT `/api/notes/1/` — update note with ID 1

DELETE `/api/notes/1/` — delete note with ID 1

No need to write those routes manually. No need to handle request parsing, data validation, or JSON serialization. DRF does it all, using simple and predictable conventions.

Now run your server:

```
python manage.py runserver
```

Open your browser and visit `http://localhost:8000/api/notes/`. What you'll see is one of DRF's best features: the **Browsable API interface**. This is a web-based interface where you can explore your API, submit data through a form, and view responses in real time. It's not just a debugging tool—it's a productivity booster during development.

At this point, what you have is a functioning REST API for your `Note` model. You can create notes from the frontend, retrieve them via AJAX calls, or use them as part of a mobile app backend.

This example is deliberately simple, but the pattern scales. DRF supports complex data structures, nested serialization, custom validation rules, token-based authentication, permissions, filtering, pagination, throttling, and more.

It is powerful enough for high-traffic APIs serving millions of users, but it's also approachable enough to learn incrementally.

In short, Django gives you the structure and power to build any backend. Django REST Framework adds the tools you need to build a **clean, maintainable, standards-compliant API**. These tools are not bolted on—they're thoughtfully integrated into Django's ecosystem.

Setting Up Your Development Environment

Before you begin building any Django-based API, you need a solid, predictable environment that lets you focus on writing code without worrying about system conflicts, missing dependencies, or accidental changes to global settings. Setting up your development environment correctly at the beginning saves you hours of debugging and unexpected behavior later on. This step is not just procedural—it's foundational to working smoothly with Django and Django REST Framework.

Let's start from the ground up, making sure everything is installed correctly and isolated so that your project can grow in a stable, controlled setup.

You'll need Python installed on your system. Django and DRF both run on Python, and most systems today come with it pre-installed. But what really matters is the version. To avoid compatibility issues, it's best to use Python 3.10 or newer, as Django 4.x and above are built and tested with those versions. If you're unsure what version you have, run the following command in your terminal:

```
python --version
```
If your system uses `python3` instead of `python`, then use:

```
python3 --version
```

If your version is outdated, install the latest version from https://www.python.org/downloads/. Once Python is in place, the next tool you need is `pip`, Python's package manager. It usually comes bundled with Python itself. You'll use `pip` to install Django, Django REST Framework, and other dependencies as your project evolves.

Now, rather than installing these libraries directly into your global Python installation, you should always isolate them inside a **virtual environment**. This creates a dedicated Python environment for your project where packages are installed locally, without affecting anything else on your system. It also means you can define project-specific dependencies in a `requirements.txt` file that others can use to reproduce the same environment exactly.

To create a virtual environment, navigate to your project folder (or create one) and run:

```
python -m venv venv
```

This command tells Python to create a virtual environment in a directory named `venv`. You can name it something else, but `venv` is a widely recognized convention.

Once it's created, you need to activate it.

On macOS and Linux:

```
source venv/bin/activate
```

On Windows (Command Prompt):

```
venv\Scripts\activate
```

On Windows (PowerShell):

```
venv\Scripts\Activate.ps1
```

When the environment is activated, you'll see your prompt change, usually prefixed with `(venv)` to show you're now operating inside the virtual environment.

Now it's time to install Django and Django REST Framework. With the environment active, run:

```
pip install django djangorestframework
```

This installs both frameworks into your virtual environment, not your global Python installation. That distinction is critical because it protects your system from conflicts and allows you to manage versions independently per project.

Once these are installed, it's a good practice to freeze your dependencies into a `requirements.txt` file:

```
pip freeze > requirements.txt
```

This file records exactly which versions were installed, which makes it easy for others to install the same versions by running:

```
pip install -r requirements.txt
```

Now you're ready to create your Django project. This is the outer container that will hold your API, its configuration, and the apps you build inside it. Run the following command:

```
django-admin startproject apibook .
```

Notice the dot at the end of the command. It tells Django to create the project in the current directory rather than nesting it one level deeper. The project will be called `apibook`, and inside it, you'll find the core files: `settings.py`, `urls.py`, `wsgi.py`, and `asgi.py`.

To verify the setup worked, start the development server:

```
python manage.py runserver
```

You should see output confirming that Django started successfully and is listening at `http://127.0.0.1:8000/`. Open that address in your browser, and you'll see Django's default welcome screen—confirmation that your project is ready.

Now let's configure your project to use Django REST Framework. Open `settings.py` and locate the `INSTALLED_APPS` list. Add `'rest_framework'` to the list like this:

```python
INSTALLED_APPS = [
    'django.contrib.admin',
    'django.contrib.auth',
    'django.contrib.contenttypes',
    'django.contrib.sessions',
    'django.contrib.messages',
    'django.contrib.staticfiles',
    'rest_framework',
]
```

This tells Django to include DRF's components in the project's app registry, which is necessary for features like serialization and class-based views to work.

At this stage, your environment is ready. You've created a clean Python virtual environment, installed Django and DRF, initialized your project, and verified that everything is wired correctly.

Let's go a step further and create your first app. Django projects are modular—each logical area of your application should live inside its own app. Run this command:

```
python manage.py startapp core
```

This creates a new folder called `core` with files for models, views, tests, and more. It's where your first API code will live.

To activate this app, you also need to add it to `INSTALLED_APPS`:

```
INSTALLED_APPS = [
    ...
    'core',
]
```

With this setup, you now have a fully functioning Django environment, enhanced by Django REST Framework, isolated by a virtual environment, and structured for real-world development. From here on, you're free to start writing models, serializers, and API endpoints with confidence that your environment is clean, reproducible, and correctly configured.

As your project grows, you'll be adding dependencies, writing reusable components, and configuring environment-specific settings. But all of that depends on having this foundational setup right from the start—and now you do.

Creating Your First API Project

Now that your development environment is correctly set up, it's time to put it to work by building your very first API project using Django and Django REST Framework. This step is about creating something functional that connects models, serializers, views, and URLs in a meaningful way. It will give you a concrete foundation to build more complex features later. The goal here is not just to get something running, but to understand each part of the system as it comes together.

Let's say you want to create an API for managing notes. Each note will have a title, a body of text, and a timestamp for when it was created. This is a practical example because it's simple, but it also demonstrates key API features like creating data, listing data, retrieving a single record, updating records, and deleting them—everything that makes up a full CRUD API.

Start by working inside the app you created earlier. If you followed the previous steps, the app is likely named core. Inside core/models.py, define your first model:

```
from django.db import models

class Note(models.Model):
    title = models.CharField(max_length=255)
    content = models.TextField()
    created_at =
models.DateTimeField(auto_now_add=True)

    def __str__(self):
        return self.title
```

This Note model includes a title field, a content field for the body of the note, and a timestamp that Django will automatically populate when the note is first created. The __str__ method is there to give a human-readable name to each note in the admin interface or other parts of the Django system that represent the model as a string.

After defining the model, you need to tell Django to create the corresponding database table. This is done in two steps. First, generate the migration:

```
python manage.py makemigrations
```

Then apply it to the database:

```
python manage.py migrate
```

Now Django knows how to store notes in your database. The next step is to create a serializer. Serializers are what allow Django REST Framework to convert model instances into JSON, and vice versa. Inside core/serializers.py, write:

```
from rest_framework import serializers
from .models import Note

class NoteSerializer(serializers.ModelSerializer):
    class Meta:
        model = Note
        fields = '__all__'
```

This serializer inherits from DRF's ModelSerializer, which automatically includes all fields from the Note model. Using '__all__' in the fields list tells DRF to include every field defined on the model. You could also list them one by one if you wanted more control or needed to exclude something.

Next, create a view that will serve as the API logic. DRF's ModelViewSet gives you a fully functional API with minimal code. In core/views.py:

```
from rest_framework import viewsets
from .models import Note
from .serializers import NoteSerializer

class NoteViewSet(viewsets.ModelViewSet):
    queryset = Note.objects.all().order_by('-created_at')
    serializer_class = NoteSerializer
```

This class defines two things: the queryset, which tells DRF which data to work with, and the serializer class, which tells it how to represent that data. The order_by('-created_at') ensures that the most recent notes show up first when listing them.

Now wire this view to a URL using DRF's router system. Routers automatically generate standard RESTful URL patterns for your viewsets. In your project's main urls.py file, typically found at apibook/urls.py, add:

```
from django.contrib import admin
from django.urls import path, include
from rest_framework.routers import DefaultRouter
```

```
from core.views import NoteViewSet

router = DefaultRouter()
router.register(r'notes', NoteViewSet)

urlpatterns = [
    path('admin/', admin.site.urls),
    path('api/', include(router.urls)),
]
```

This router registers the `NoteViewSet` and creates a set of URLs under the `/api/notes/` path. At this point, you can start the development server:

```
python manage.py runserver
```

Visit http://127.0.0.1:8000/api/notes/ in your browser. What you'll see is one of the most useful features of Django REST Framework: the browsable API interface. It allows you to interact with your API directly through the browser. You can view data, submit forms to create new notes, edit existing ones, and delete them—all through an intuitive interface that's generated automatically based on your serializers and viewsets.

Now open an API testing tool such as Postman or use the `curl` command-line utility if you prefer to work from the terminal. Try sending a POST request to the same endpoint to create a new note:

```
curl -X POST http://127.0.0.1:8000/api/notes/ \
-H "Content-Type: application/json" \
-d '{"title": "First Note", "content": "This is a
test note created via API."}'
```

You should receive a JSON response with the full note object, including the new `id` and `created_at` timestamp.

This basic interaction demonstrates the full lifecycle of a resource in a RESTful API:

You created a database model to represent a real-world object.

You wrote a serializer to translate it to and from JSON.

You wrote a viewset to handle HTTP actions like GET, POST, PUT, and DELETE.

You connected the viewset to a URL using a router.

You interacted with the API through the browsable interface and through a command-line tool.

Everything you just built is real, usable, and scalable. With no extra configuration, this API can now be consumed by any frontend application—whether it's written in React, Vue, Angular, or a native mobile platform like Android or iOS. The API you've written supports data retrieval, creation, editing, and deletion, and it adheres to common REST conventions, which means it's predictable and easy to use for anyone who knows how to work with standard HTTP APIs.

You could stop here and already have something useful. But this project is only the beginning. You haven't added authentication or permissions yet. You haven't validated data beyond the field-level constraints. You haven't implemented filtering, pagination, or documentation. Those features are coming soon, and each one builds on the structure you've already created here.

This is your base. From this point forward, every concept we explore—whether it's security, testing, performance, or deployment—will relate back to the kind of structure you've just built. And because Django and DRF handle so much of the underlying complexity for you, you're free to focus on building business logic, enforcing your API design standards, and delivering useful functionality without writing repetitive boilerplate code.

Chapter 2: Designing RESTful APIs

The code you write will work. The question is: will it be usable, predictable, and easy to maintain six months from now? Will other developers be able to understand your API without asking for documentation every five minutes? Will your frontend team be able to work independently of the backend team without constantly coordinating over vague endpoints?

That's why thoughtful design matters in API development.

Designing a RESTful API is about more than just exposing database models. It's about creating a consistent, logical, and predictable interface that other software—and often other developers—can rely on. In this chapter, you'll learn how to think through your API's structure, behavior, and presentation with a mindset that prioritizes clarity, usability, and long-term maintainability.

Core Principles of REST

When you're building an API that's intended to be reliable, scalable, and easy to use, it's not enough to just expose your data over HTTP. You need to follow a set of principles that make your API consistent, predictable, and understandable—not just to you, but to any developer who might use it now or in the future. This is where REST comes in.

REST stands for **Representational State Transfer**. It's not a framework, or a technology, or a specific tool. It's a set of architectural guidelines that define how distributed systems should communicate over HTTP. And it's been around since the early 2000s, when it was introduced by Roy Fielding in his doctoral dissertation. The point of REST isn't complexity—it's clarity. It's meant to help you design APIs that behave in a uniform, resource-oriented way.

At the core of REST is the idea of **resources**. A resource is any piece of data you want to expose—users, blog posts, orders, comments, projects, tasks, products. Each of these is treated as an addressable entity that lives at a specific URL. When someone wants to access that resource, they make a request to its URL using a specific HTTP method that expresses what they want to do.

Let's take a simple example. Suppose you're building an API for a book store. You might define a resource called `Book`. Every book in your database is a resource, and each one is uniquely accessible by its ID. You might have endpoints like:

`/books/` — a collection of all books

`/books/42/` — a single book with ID 42

If a client wants to retrieve a list of all books, it sends a GET request to `/books/`. If it wants to add a new book to the collection, it sends a POST request to the same endpoint, but with a body containing the new book data. To update an existing book, it sends a PUT or PATCH request to `/books/42/`. To delete that book, it sends a DELETE request to the same URL.

This design is not only clean—it also aligns perfectly with how the HTTP protocol was intended to work. You're not inventing new verbs or actions. You're using the web's own language.

Here's how a Django REST Framework implementation might look for this resource:

```python
# models.py
from django.db import models

class Book(models.Model):
    title = models.CharField(max_length=255)
    author = models.CharField(max_length=255)
    published_date = models.DateField()
    isbn = models.CharField(max_length=13)

    def __str__(self):
        return self.title
# serializers.py
from rest_framework import serializers
from .models import Book

class BookSerializer(serializers.ModelSerializer):
    class Meta:
        model = Book
        fields = '__all__'
# views.py
```

```python
from rest_framework import viewsets
from .models import Book
from .serializers import BookSerializer

class BookViewSet(viewsets.ModelViewSet):
    queryset = Book.objects.all()
    serializer_class = BookSerializer
# urls.py
from rest_framework.routers import DefaultRouter
from .views import BookViewSet

router = DefaultRouter()
router.register(r'books', BookViewSet)

urlpatterns = [
    path('api/', include(router.urls)),
]
```

What this gives you is a fully functional RESTful API for your `Book` resource:

`GET /api/books/` returns a list of all books.

`POST /api/books/` allows you to add a new book.

`GET /api/books/5/` retrieves the book with ID 5.

`PUT /api/books/5/` updates the full record.

`PATCH /api/books/5/` updates part of the record.

`DELETE /api/books/5/` removes the book.

You're not writing extra code to handle every route. You're relying on the REST framework to give each resource a uniform interface. This uniformity is one of REST's most powerful ideas. It means that once someone understands how one resource works, they can use all the others in the same way. That reduces friction and makes your API easier to work with, especially in large systems.

REST also emphasizes **statelessness**. This means that each request from the client must contain all the information needed to understand and process that request. The server does not store session information between requests. If a client sends a request to `GET /books/`, the server doesn't rely on any prior context to understand what the request is for. It uses the request alone to determine how to respond.

This has a few very real benefits. Stateless APIs are easier to scale. You can run multiple API servers behind a load balancer, and any one of them can process any request independently. There's no need for server-side session memory, and this makes load distribution far simpler. Statelessness also improves testability and reliability because you know that each request can be evaluated on its own, without worrying about previous state.

Let's say you're building an authentication system on top of your REST API. Because of REST's stateless nature, you don't use sessions stored on the server. Instead, you issue a token to the client after login, and the client sends that token with every request—usually in the Authorization header. This is consistent with REST's statelessness, and it works across servers, clients, and even external applications.

Here's a basic example using token authentication in DRF:

```
# First, install the DRF token auth package if
needed
pip install djangorestframework
```

Then enable it in settings.py:

```
INSTALLED_APPS = [
    ...
    'rest_framework',
    'rest_framework.authtoken',
]
```

Run the migrations to create the token model:

```
python manage.py migrate
```

In your settings:

```
REST_FRAMEWORK = {
    'DEFAULT_AUTHENTICATION_CLASSES': [

'rest_framework.authentication.TokenAuthentication'
,
    ]
```

```
}
```

Create a view for generating tokens:

```
from rest_framework.authtoken.views import
obtain_auth_token

urlpatterns = [
    path('api/token/', obtain_auth_token,
name='api_token_auth'),
]
```

Now when a user sends a POST request to /api/token/ with their username and password, the API responds with a token. The client must send that token in the Authorization header on every request:

```
Authorization: Token
94a3c1f7ac1548c193cce4e73469adf1a8c5a441
```

Each request is stateless—independent from the one before—and yet secure and authenticated.

Another principle REST promotes is **cacheability**. Because REST responses are typically structured around specific resources and do not depend on session state, they can be cached by clients and proxies. This improves performance, especially when dealing with data that doesn't change frequently, such as product catalogs or article archives.

If your API endpoint returns data that is safe to cache, you can add appropriate headers to your response using DRF's middleware or custom view logic. This allows downstream systems to avoid hitting your API on every request, reducing load and latency.

Lastly, REST supports a **layered architecture**. Your client doesn't need to know whether it's talking to the actual backend server, a reverse proxy, a gateway, or a load balancer. The architecture encourages separation of concerns. Authentication, logging, load balancing, and business logic can all live in separate layers. This helps teams scale their infrastructure and enforce consistent policies.

In practical terms, this means you can use tools like Nginx to rate-limit or log traffic without touching your Django code. Or you can use API gateways like Kong or AWS API Gateway to apply policies globally, while your application logic stays focused on delivering data.

So when you follow REST principles—resource orientation, statelessness, uniform interfaces, cacheability, and layered architecture—you're not just writing an API that works. You're writing an API that others can understand, rely on, and build around confidently.

And in today's development landscape, where APIs are the foundation of almost every digital product, that level of clarity and reliability is not a luxury. It's a necessity.

Resource Modeling and Endpoint Planning

When you're designing an API, the first thing you need to get right is your understanding of the data you're exposing. Every piece of data in your system—whether it's a user, a product, a comment, or a task—should be treated as a resource. And every resource should be designed with care.

Let's start from the beginning. Before writing any code, you need to think about the nouns in your system. These nouns are your potential resources. You're not designing function calls, and you're not exposing internal database tables. You're presenting meaningful entities to the outside world in a stable and logical way.

Suppose you're building a simple task management API, something similar to Trello or Asana. The core objects users will interact with might include:

Projects

Tasks

Users

Comments

Labels

Each of these is a resource. And each resource will need a URL where it can be accessed, methods to operate on it, and a data format to represent it. This is the heart of resource modeling: defining the structure and relationships of each resource and how it will behave over HTTP.

Start with one: the `Project`. A project contains metadata like a name, a description, a start and end date, and probably a list of tasks. In your Django models, you might begin like this:

```
# core/models.py
from django.db import models

class Project(models.Model):
    name = models.CharField(max_length=100)
    description = models.TextField(blank=True)
    start_date = models.DateField()
    end_date = models.DateField()

    def __str__(self):
        return self.name
```

Now add a `Task` model that is related to a project. This relationship is critical because it defines how resources connect to each other, and that connection shapes your API's endpoint structure.

```
class Task(models.Model):
    project = models.ForeignKey(Project,
on_delete=models.CASCADE, related_name='tasks')
    title = models.CharField(max_length=100)
    is_completed =
models.BooleanField(default=False)
    due_date = models.DateField(null=True,
blank=True)

    def __str__(self):
        return self.title
```

Now you have two related models. The next step is to decide how to expose them over the API. This is where endpoint planning comes into play.

You'll want to expose both projects and tasks as top-level resources. This means a client should be able to request a list of all projects using

34

`/api/projects/`, retrieve a specific project with `/api/projects/1/`, and do the same for tasks at `/api/tasks/` and `/api/tasks/1/`.

But because tasks are tied to a specific project, it's also useful to provide a nested endpoint that shows only the tasks related to a particular project. That might look like `/api/projects/1/tasks/`.

This dual exposure—both top-level and nested—is common in REST APIs. The top-level endpoint is for general access, and the nested endpoint helps with filtering by parent resource. In Django REST Framework, you can accomplish both.

Let's start by creating serializers:

```python
# core/serializers.py
from rest_framework import serializers
from .models import Project, Task

class TaskSerializer(serializers.ModelSerializer):
    class Meta:
        model = Task
        fields = '__all__'

class
ProjectSerializer(serializers.ModelSerializer):
    tasks = TaskSerializer(many=True,
read_only=True)

    class Meta:
        model = Project
        fields = '__all__'
```

In this example, the `ProjectSerializer` includes a read-only list of tasks, thanks to the `related_name='tasks'` on the `Task` model's ForeignKey. This allows the client to view all tasks associated with a project in a single call.

Now define your views:

```python
# core/views.py
from rest_framework import viewsets
from .models import Project, Task
```

```
from .serializers import ProjectSerializer,
TaskSerializer

class ProjectViewSet(viewsets.ModelViewSet):
    queryset = Project.objects.all()
    serializer_class = ProjectSerializer

class TaskViewSet(viewsets.ModelViewSet):
    queryset = Task.objects.all()
    serializer_class = TaskSerializer
```

At this point, if you register these viewsets with Django REST Framework's default router, you'll have two top-level routes:

```
/api/projects/
```

```
/api/tasks/
```

But what if you want to include nested routes like `/api/projects/1/tasks/`? For that, you'll need to use **nested routers**. You can achieve this using a third-party package like `drf-nested-routers`.

Install it:

```
pip install drf-nested-routers
```

Then update your `urls.py`:

```
from rest_framework_nested import routers
from core.views import ProjectViewSet, TaskViewSet

router = routers.DefaultRouter()
router.register(r'projects', ProjectViewSet,
basename='project')

projects_router =
routers.NestedDefaultRouter(router, r'projects',
lookup='project')
projects_router.register(r'tasks', TaskViewSet,
basename='project-tasks')

urlpatterns = [
    path('api/', include(router.urls)),
    path('api/', include(projects_router.urls)),
```

]

With this setup, your API now supports both:

`/api/tasks/` — all tasks across all projects

`/api/projects/3/tasks/` — tasks for project with ID 3

Inside your `TaskViewSet`, you can use the `project_pk` from the nested route to filter tasks accordingly:

```
def get_queryset(self):
    if 'project_pk' in self.kwargs:
        return
Task.objects.filter(project_id=self.kwargs['project
_pk'])
    return Task.objects.all()
```

This approach respects the relationships in your data model, while giving clients flexible ways to access and organize their data.

You might be wondering—why not just expose one version and avoid the complexity? The reason is usability. Different consumers of your API have different needs. A dashboard UI might want to fetch all tasks at once, while a mobile app viewing a single project will only want tasks related to that one project. Giving both access paths keeps your API flexible and practical.

Good resource modeling isn't just about making things work. It's about anticipating how your API will be used, and designing it so that those common use cases are fast, easy, and intuitive.

When planning your endpoints, always ground your thinking in the real structure of your data. Use relationships in your models to shape your URLs. Present resources as nouns, not actions. Let the structure of your application guide your API design, and always aim for clarity over cleverness.

Your endpoints are the front door to your system. Plan them with the same care you'd give to the data they expose. If the structure is thoughtful, the rest of your API development process will be far smoother—for you and for anyone who has to use what you've built.

URI Conventions, HTTP Methods, and Status Codes

When you build a REST API, you're essentially designing a public interface—something that other software, systems, and developers will interact with. That interface is made up of three tightly connected pieces: **URIs**, **HTTP methods**, and **status codes**. Each one plays a distinct role in how your API communicates. When used correctly, they make your API feel intuitive, predictable, and reliable. When used poorly, they introduce confusion and bugs.

Let's start by talking about **URIs**, or Uniform Resource Identifiers. These are the paths clients use to access specific resources in your system. They're like addresses on the web that point to your data. A common mistake is treating URIs like action commands. For example, creating endpoints like `/getAllUsers`, `/deleteUserById`, or `/createNewOrder`. These feel natural if you're coming from an RPC or controller-based mindset, but they don't follow REST principles.

In REST, your URIs should represent **resources**, not actions. Think in terms of nouns, not verbs. A resource is a thing—users, products, comments—not an operation. The action part of the interaction is expressed through the HTTP method, not in the URI.

So instead of designing something like `/deleteUserById`, you expose the resource at `/users/123/`, and if a client wants to delete it, they send a `DELETE` request to that URL. The verb is the HTTP method, and the noun is the URI. This separation of concerns is a fundamental principle in REST.

Here's how it works in a Django REST Framework project. Suppose you have a `User` model and a `UserViewSet`. If you register it with DRF's router:

```python
# core/views.py
from rest_framework import viewsets
from .models import User
from .serializers import UserSerializer

class UserViewSet(viewsets.ModelViewSet):
```

38

```
    queryset = User.objects.all()
    serializer_class = UserSerializer
# core/urls.py
from rest_framework.routers import DefaultRouter
from .views import UserViewSet

router = DefaultRouter()
router.register(r'users', UserViewSet)

urlpatterns = [
    path('api/', include(router.urls)),
]
```

This setup automatically gives you these resource-based URIs:

GET /api/users/ – fetch all users

POST /api/users/ – create a new user

GET /api/users/5/ – retrieve user with ID 5

PUT /api/users/5/ – fully update user with ID 5

PATCH /api/users/5/ – partially update user with ID 5

DELETE /api/users/5/ – delete user with ID 5

These are all clean, consistent, and intuitive. No extra code required. The URI tells you what you're working with. The HTTP method tells you what you want to do with it.

Let's go deeper into HTTP methods, because they're the verbs of your API. The five most commonly used methods in RESTful APIs are GET, POST, PUT, PATCH, and DELETE. Each one maps to a standard CRUD operation.

Use GET when you want to read data. It should be safe and idempotent. That means a GET request doesn't change any data, and making the same GET request multiple times will always return the same result (unless the data has changed on its own).

Use POST when you want to create a new resource. This method is **not idempotent**. If you POST the same data twice, you'll likely end up with two records.

Use PUT to replace a resource entirely. You provide a full set of fields, and the server replaces the old resource with the new one. It's **idempotent**, meaning multiple identical PUT requests will produce the same result.

Use PATCH when you want to partially update a resource. You only send the fields you want to update. PATCH is also idempotent.

Use DELETE when you want to remove a resource. The request might return a confirmation or simply an empty response.

These methods are supported natively by Django REST Framework's viewsets. You don't need to manually configure anything unless you want to override the default behavior.

Let's take an example. Suppose you want to update only the email field of a user. With DRF and PATCH, you could send a request like this:

```
PATCH /api/users/12/
Content-Type: application/json

{
   "email": "new.email@example.com"
}
```

DRF will validate the input and update just the email field. The rest of the user's data remains unchanged. If instead you used PUT, you would need to send all fields:

```
PUT /api/users/12/
Content-Type: application/json

{
   "username": "existing_user",
   "email": "new.email@example.com",
   "is_active": true
}
```

If you omit a field in PUT, DRF will typically consider it null or raise a validation error, depending on your serializer configuration. This is why PUT is used when replacing, and PATCH is preferred for partial updates.

Now let's talk about status codes. Every response from your API should include a meaningful HTTP status code. These codes are critical—they let the client know what happened. Was the request successful? Did the user provide invalid input? Did the server fail?

Let's go through what these status codes actually mean in practice.

When a client successfully retrieves data with a GET request, the API should return a 200 OK response. This is the baseline success response. For a successful POST that creates a resource, use 201 Created. And include the new resource in the response body—often including the id and a full representation of the created object.

For example:

```
{
   "id": 8,
   "username": "jane_doe",
   "email": "jane@example.com"
}
```

If the client deletes a resource, you typically return 204 No Content to signal that the operation succeeded, but there's no additional data to return.

Validation errors should return a 400 Bad Request response. DRF handles this for you out of the box. If a required field is missing, or if a value doesn't match the serializer's validation logic, DRF will raise a ValidationError, and the response will include the relevant error messages:

```
{
   "email": ["This field is required."]
}
```

Authentication failures should return 401 Unauthorized. This means the client either didn't provide a valid token or provided none at all. If a user is authenticated but doesn't have permission to access a resource, return 403 Forbidden.

If the resource doesn't exist—say the client requests /api/users/999/—the API should respond with 404 Not Found. Don't return a blank 200 OK. That's misleading and causes client-side errors.

Server errors—issues you didn't anticipate, like a bug in your code or a database outage—should return 500 Internal Server Error. Django handles these automatically unless you intercept them.

You can also customize status codes in your views. Let's say you want to return 202 Accepted for an asynchronous background job:

```
from rest_framework.response import Response
from rest_framework import status

def trigger_background_job(request):
    # logic to queue job
    return Response({"message": "Job accepted"},
status=status.HTTP_202_ACCEPTED)
```

By setting the correct status code, you give your API consumers the information they need to handle the response properly.

Let's bring it all together with an example.

You have a task management API. A client wants to create a new task. They send:

```
POST /api/tasks/
Content-Type: application/json

{
  "title": "Write chapter on status codes",
  "due_date": "2025-04-05"
}
```

If the input is valid, your API responds with:

```
201 Created
{
  "id": 14,
  "title": "Write chapter on status codes",
  "due_date": "2025-04-05",
  "is_completed": false
}
```

If they forget to include the title, DRF responds with:

```
400 Bad Request
```

```
{
  "title": ["This field is required."]
}
```

If they try to update a task that doesn't exist:

```
404 Not Found
```

These conventions make your API self-documenting. Anyone working with it doesn't need to guess what status code to expect or what method to use—they can rely on industry standards.

By following these principles—clear URIs, consistent use of HTTP methods, and appropriate status codes—you create an API that behaves predictably, communicates effectively, and integrates smoothly into any environment.

API Versioning Strategies

When you first release an API, things are simple. You have a handful of endpoints, you know exactly how your resources are structured, and your frontend or external clients work seamlessly with the current contract. But as time passes, you'll inevitably need to make changes. Maybe you want to restructure a response, rename a field, improve performance, or introduce a new feature that requires a modified data format.

If you're not versioning your API, every change you make has the potential to **break someone else's code**. That someone could be a customer, another developer on your team, or even yourself six months later.

API versioning is how you manage change **safely**. It allows you to evolve your API over time while still maintaining stability for existing users who depend on the older behavior. When done right, versioning provides a clear upgrade path, makes it easy to support legacy clients, and gives you the freedom to improve your API without fear.

There are different strategies for versioning your API. The key is to pick one that fits your use case and enforce it consistently.

The most common and widely accepted method is **URL path versioning**. This involves including the version number directly in the URL of every endpoint. It's visible, it's explicit, and it's very easy to route in most web frameworks.

For example, instead of:

`/api/users/`

You'd use:

`/api/v1/users/`

Later, if you need to change the structure of your user resource, you can introduce a new version without breaking clients that depend on the old one:

`/api/v2/users/`

Each version lives side by side, and you can deprecate older versions gradually.

In Django REST Framework, setting this up is straightforward using **namespaces** and optional versioning classes.

Let's walk through a complete example. Start by creating separate modules for each version of your API. For simplicity, let's keep v1 and v2 in different subdirectories of your app.

Your project structure might look like this:

```
core/
├── v1/
│   ├── views.py
│   ├── serializers.py
│   └── urls.py
├── v2/
│   ├── views.py
│   ├── serializers.py
│   └── urls.py
│
```

In `core/v1/views.py`, define a viewset:

```
from rest_framework import viewsets
from .serializers import UserSerializer
from ..models import User

class UserViewSetV1(viewsets.ModelViewSet):
    queryset = User.objects.all()
    serializer_class = UserSerializer
```

In `core/v2/views.py`, maybe you want to exclude a deprecated field, or include new computed data:

```
from rest_framework import viewsets
from .serializers import UserSerializer
from ..models import User

class UserViewSetV2(viewsets.ModelViewSet):
    queryset = User.objects.all()
    serializer_class = UserSerializer
```

Your serializers in `v1/serializers.py` and `v2/serializers.py` can differ based on what you want each version to expose. Maybe version 2 adds a `full_name` field and omits an old field you no longer want to support:

```
# v1/serializers.py
from rest_framework import serializers
from ..models import User

class UserSerializer(serializers.ModelSerializer):
    class Meta:
        model = User
        fields = ['id', 'username', 'email',
'date_joined']
# v2/serializers.py
from rest_framework import serializers
from ..models import User

class UserSerializer(serializers.ModelSerializer):
    full_name = serializers.SerializerMethodField()

    class Meta:
        model = User
```

```
        fields = ['id', 'username', 'full_name']

    def get_full_name(self, obj):
        return f"{obj.first_name} {obj.last_name}"
```

Then define separate routers and URL configs:

```
# core/v1/urls.py
from rest_framework.routers import DefaultRouter
from .views import UserViewSetV1

router = DefaultRouter()
router.register(r'users', UserViewSetV1)

urlpatterns = router.urls
# core/v2/urls.py
from rest_framework.routers import DefaultRouter
from .views import UserViewSetV2

router = DefaultRouter()
router.register(r'users', UserViewSetV2)

urlpatterns = router.urls
```

Now, in your project's main `urls.py`, include both versions with their respective namespaces:

```
from django.urls import path, include

urlpatterns = [
    path('api/v1/', include(('core.v1.urls', 'v1'),
namespace='v1')),
    path('api/v2/', include(('core.v2.urls', 'v2'),
namespace='v2')),
]
```

That's all you need to support multiple versions of your API. Clients using version 1 can continue calling `/api/v1/users/`, and clients ready to use version 2 can switch to `/api/v2/users/`. The two can coexist peacefully, and you can decide when it's appropriate to phase out old versions.

If you want to enforce or inspect versioning at the request level, you can use DRF's built-in versioning support. For example, you can enable `NamespaceVersioning` like this:

```python
# settings.py
REST_FRAMEWORK = {
    'DEFAULT_VERSIONING_CLASS':
'rest_framework.versioning.NamespaceVersioning',
}
```

With this in place, you can inspect the request version in your views:

```python
def list(self, request, *args, **kwargs):
    version = request.version
    if version == 'v2':
        # do something custom
    return super().list(request, *args, **kwargs)
```

This is helpful when you need fine-grained control, such as when multiple versions share a base viewset but vary in behavior.

Another strategy is **header-based versioning**. In this model, the client specifies the desired version using a custom header, like:

```
Accept: application/vnd.myapp.v2+json
```

Or:

```
X-API-Version: 2
```

While this keeps your URLs clean, it requires every client to manage request headers carefully. This approach is often used in APIs where clean URLs are critical or when using advanced API gateways. In Django REST Framework, you can support it by switching the versioning class:

```python
REST_FRAMEWORK = {
    'DEFAULT_VERSIONING_CLASS':
'rest_framework.versioning.AcceptHeaderVersioning',
    'DEFAULT_VERSION': 'v1',
    'ALLOWED_VERSIONS': ['v1', 'v2'],
    'VERSION_PARAM': 'version',
}
```

There's also **query parameter versioning**, where the client appends `?version=v2` to the request. This method is easy to implement and test, but it clutters the URL and isn't widely adopted in large-scale production APIs. You can enable it using:

```
REST_FRAMEWORK = {
    'DEFAULT_VERSIONING_CLASS':
'rest_framework.versioning.QueryParameterVersioning
',
    'VERSION_PARAM': 'version',
}
```

For most cases, **URL path versioning** is the most practical and clear method. It requires no special configuration from the client, integrates easily with routers and namespaces, and makes version intent visible to developers and users inspecting the API.

Whichever strategy you choose, the most important thing is to **commit to it early** and be consistent. Inconsistencies in versioning will lead to confusion, especially as your API grows and your client base expands. You should also document which versions are supported, what the default version is, and how long each version will be maintained before deprecation.

Good versioning protects your users from change, gives your team room to grow the product, and communicates clearly what each part of the API is supposed to do at any given time. It's not a technical burden—it's a promise that your API won't surprise the people who rely on it. And in software, that kind of trust is worth more than almost anything else.

Documenting Design with OpenAPI and Swagger

When you build an API, writing code is only part of the job. What really determines whether others can successfully use your API—especially other developers—is the **quality of your documentation**. A well-structured, consistent API is only as useful as its discoverability. If someone can't understand how to interact with your endpoints, what fields are required, or what data formats are expected, your API becomes a guessing game.

This is where **OpenAPI** and **Swagger** come in. They provide a standard, machine-readable way to describe your API—its endpoints, data models, parameters, authentication methods, and responses. That description can then be used to generate interactive documentation, code samples, and API clients automatically.

Let's break this down clearly.

OpenAPI is the specification. It defines the format and structure of the documentation in YAML or JSON. **Swagger UI** is one of the most popular tools built on top of OpenAPI—it takes that machine-readable spec and turns it into a dynamic, interactive, web-based API explorer.

In Django REST Framework, documentation support used to be limited or heavily manual. Thankfully, this has improved drastically. The most reliable and well-maintained way to generate an OpenAPI spec in DRF is with a package called **drf-spectacular**. It integrates seamlessly with DRF and generates accurate, modern OpenAPI 3 schemas.

Let's walk through the complete setup.

Start by installing the package:

```
pip install drf-spectacular
```

Then add it to your Django settings. In your `settings.py` file, configure it like this:

```
REST_FRAMEWORK = {
    'DEFAULT_SCHEMA_CLASS':
'drf_spectacular.openapi.AutoSchema',
}
```

This tells DRF to use `drf-spectacular` to generate your schema instead of the built-in legacy system.

Now, you need to expose the generated schema via a URL. You can do this in your `urls.py` file:

```
from django.urls import path
from drf_spectacular.views import
SpectacularAPIView, SpectacularSwaggerView
```

```
urlpatterns = [
    path('api/schema/',
SpectacularAPIView.as_view(), name='schema'),
    path('api/docs/',
SpectacularSwaggerView.as_view(url_name='schema'),
name='swagger-ui'),
]
```

With this in place, visit /api/docs/ in your browser. What you'll see is Swagger UI—a dynamic, interactive API explorer. Every endpoint in your API is listed there. You can click on it, see what parameters it expects, view example responses, and even send real API requests from the browser.

Let's say you've created a view like this:

```
from rest_framework import viewsets
from .models import Task
from .serializers import TaskSerializer

class TaskViewSet(viewsets.ModelViewSet):
    queryset = Task.objects.all()
    serializer_class = TaskSerializer
```

With the schema and Swagger UI configured, this viewset will automatically appear in your documentation. You don't have to write anything extra. It will list:

The available methods (GET, POST, PUT, PATCH, DELETE)

The required fields for each method

The response format

Status codes like 200, 201, 400, 404

If you want to customize or enhance the generated documentation, drf-spectacular supports that as well. You can add descriptions to serializers, methods, and fields, and those will be reflected in the Swagger UI.

Here's how you can document a field in a serializer:

```
from rest_framework import serializers
from .models import Task
```

```python
class TaskSerializer(serializers.ModelSerializer):
    title = serializers.CharField(help_text="Title
of the task (required, max 100 chars)")
    description =
serializers.CharField(help_text="Detailed
description of the task")

    class Meta:
        model = Task
        fields = '__all__'
```

Now, when someone looks at the POST /tasks/ endpoint in your Swagger UI, they'll see those help texts as part of the input field documentation. This makes it clear what the client is supposed to send, without needing to guess or refer to your source code.

You can also annotate your views or viewsets to add summaries, tags, and more. For example:

```python
from drf_spectacular.utils import extend_schema,
OpenApiParameter
from rest_framework.viewsets import ModelViewSet

@extend_schema(
    summary="List all tasks",
    description="Returns a paginated list of all
tasks. Supports filtering by project ID.",
    parameters=[
        OpenApiParameter(name='project', type=int,
location=OpenApiParameter.QUERY,
description='Filter by project ID')
    ]
)
class TaskViewSet(ModelViewSet):
    ...
```

This annotation adds a summary and parameter documentation that will be displayed in your Swagger UI. Now, your API isn't just functional—it's self-describing and informative.

Let's take it one step further. What if you want to generate a static version of your API documentation to be bundled with your release or included in a third-party SDK? `drf-spectacular` can export the OpenAPI spec to a file:

```
python manage.py spectacular --file schema.yaml
```

You now have a complete YAML schema file describing your entire API. You can check it into version control, use it with API gateways, or pass it to tools that generate client SDKs in Python, JavaScript, Go, and more.

Good documentation is not something you leave until the end. It's not just a README or a PDF file. It's something that grows with your API, right alongside the views and serializers. By integrating OpenAPI generation into your development process from the beginning, you ensure your documentation is always up to date, always accurate, and always available to anyone who needs it.

And more than that—it sends a message. It tells your users that you care about quality. That your API is a product, not just an interface. That you want them to succeed when integrating with your system.

That kind of clarity and professionalism will save you support requests, reduce integration bugs, and improve adoption—whether you're working on an internal tool or a public platform.

So treat your API documentation as a first-class part of your development process. Use OpenAPI. Expose Swagger UI. Keep it accurate. And above all, make sure your API tells the truth about how it behaves, so the people who rely on it can do their work with confidence.

Chapter 3: Building Your Data Layer with Django Models

When building APIs, everything starts with data. If your models are clean, consistent, and well-structured, then your serializers, views, and endpoints will follow that same clarity. But if your models are messy, inconsistent, or under-specified, you'll spend the rest of your project fighting unexpected behaviors, confusing bugs, and edge cases that shouldn't exist in the first place.

In this chapter, we're going to focus on building a strong foundation for your API by writing clean, meaningful Django models. We'll walk through practical examples, cover best practices, and ensure your models reflect the real-world entities your application is supposed to represent.

Modeling Real-World Data with Django ORM

The core of any web application is its data. Whether you're building an API for a library, a logistics platform, or a food delivery service, the way you represent your data in the system determines how effective and maintainable your code will be. This is why your data modeling decisions deserve your full attention, especially when working with Django.

Django's **ORM (Object-Relational Mapper)** is what connects your Python classes to your relational database tables. With it, you define models in Python, and Django handles the SQL behind the scenes. This not only makes development faster and more readable, but it also ensures your data is structured consistently.

Let's walk through a real-world example.

Say you're building an API for a course management system. You'll need to represent things like students, courses, instructors, and enrollments. Each of these is a separate concept—what Django would call a **model**.

You start by identifying the key pieces of data and their attributes. For a `Course`, you might need a title, a description, a course code, and a publication status.

Here's what the model might look like:

```python
# core/models.py

from django.db import models

class Course(models.Model):
    title = models.CharField(max_length=255)
    code = models.CharField(max_length=20,
unique=True)
    description = models.TextField(blank=True)
    is_published =
models.BooleanField(default=False)
    created_at =
models.DateTimeField(auto_now_add=True)

    def __str__(self):
        return f"{self.code} - {self.title}"
```

Every field here maps to a column in the corresponding database table. `CharField` and `TextField` represent short and long text respectively. `BooleanField` represents true/false flags. `DateTimeField` captures timestamps.

The `__str__()` method is not required, but it's strongly recommended. When Django refers to an instance—whether in the admin panel, logs, or shell—it will call this method. Without it, you'd just see "Course object (3)," which tells you nothing. With a string method that includes the code and title, you immediately get context.

Once your model is defined, you need to create a migration for it:

```
python manage.py makemigrations
```

This generates a migration file that records the structure of your model. Then apply it:

```
python manage.py migrate
```

At this point, your `Course` model is stored in the database, and you can begin creating and querying course records directly using Django's ORM.

Let's create a course in the Django shell:

```
python manage.py shell
```

Then run:

```
from core.models import Course

Course.objects.create(
    title="REST API Development with Django",
    code="API101",
    description="A practical course on building
RESTful APIs using Django and DRF.",
    is_published=True
)
```

Django translates this into a SQL INSERT statement and stores the record in your database.

You can fetch all published courses like this:

```
Course.objects.filter(is_published=True)
```

Or retrieve a specific course by code:

```
Course.objects.get(code="API101")
```

If you make a typo or search for a course that doesn't exist, Django will raise a DoesNotExist exception. This is useful for debugging and control flow in your views or services.

Modeling with Django ORM gives you the ability to build queries using Python syntax that's both expressive and safe. You don't have to worry about SQL injection, and the queries are optimized under the hood for most use cases.

Let's extend our model with a Student:

```
class Student(models.Model):
    first_name = models.CharField(max_length=100)
    last_name = models.CharField(max_length=100)
    email = models.EmailField(unique=True)
    enrolled_at =
models.DateTimeField(auto_now_add=True)

    def __str__(self):
```

```
        return f"{self.first_name}
{self.last_name}"
```

And now, a many-to-many relationship between students and courses:

```
class Enrollment(models.Model):
    student = models.ForeignKey(Student,
on_delete=models.CASCADE,
related_name='enrollments')
    course = models.ForeignKey(Course,
on_delete=models.CASCADE,
related_name='enrollments')
    enrolled_on =
models.DateTimeField(auto_now_add=True)

    class Meta:
        unique_together = ('student', 'course')

    def __str__(self):
        return f"{self.student} enrolled in
{self.course.code}"
```

This structure reflects a real-world relationship. One student can enroll in many courses. One course can have many students. The `Enrollment` model acts as a bridge table, storing additional metadata like the enrollment date. The `unique_together` constraint enforces that a student can't be enrolled in the same course more than once.

To query this data, you might write:

```
# Get all students enrolled in a course
course = Course.objects.get(code="API101")
students =
Student.objects.filter(enrollments__course=course)

# Get all courses for a student
student =
Student.objects.get(email="student@example.com")
courses =
Course.objects.filter(enrollments__student=student)
```

These reverse relationships are made possible by the `related_name` you specify on your `ForeignKey`. They give you a clean and efficient way to traverse the relationships in both directions.

And this is where the power of Django's ORM becomes clear. You're not writing raw SQL or manually handling joins. You're using intuitive, Pythonic syntax that reflects the actual structure of your data.

As your application grows, the data models you define here will be the foundation for serializers, views, permissions, and business logic. So take your time. Model your real-world entities carefully. Focus on relationships, constraints, and clarity. Don't treat your models as just a way to persist data. Treat them as the backbone of your application—and design them with the same care you'd give to your public API.

Managing Relationships and Constraints

In the real world, data is rarely isolated. A course has many students. A product belongs to a category. An invoice references a customer. When you build APIs that reflect real business processes, your models need to represent these relationships clearly and safely. That's where Django's relational modeling features and constraints come into play.

Django's ORM gives you the tools to define **relationships** directly in your models using `ForeignKey`, `OneToOneField`, and `ManyToManyField`. These fields aren't just about linking models—they help express your application's logic and enforce important rules at the database level.

Let's take a practical example. Say you're building an API for an online course platform. You have courses, instructors, students, and enrollments.

Start with the `Instructor` and `Course` models. Each course is created by one instructor, but each instructor can teach multiple courses. That's a classic **one-to-many** relationship.

```
# core/models.py

from django.db import models
```

```python
class Instructor(models.Model):
    full_name = models.CharField(max_length=150)
    bio = models.TextField(blank=True)

    def __str__(self):
        return self.full_name

class Course(models.Model):
    title = models.CharField(max_length=255)
    description = models.TextField()
    instructor = models.ForeignKey(Instructor,
on_delete=models.CASCADE, related_name='courses')

    def __str__(self):
        return self.title
```

The `ForeignKey` field in `Course` creates the relationship. The `related_name='courses'` allows you to easily access all courses taught by an instructor like this:

```python
instructor = Instructor.objects.get(id=1)
instructor_courses = instructor.courses.all()
```

This relationship also helps Django optimize queries through `select_related` and `prefetch_related`, which you can use later for performance tuning.

Now let's add students and their enrollments. A student can enroll in many courses, and each course can have many students. That's a **many-to-many** relationship.

You could use Django's `ManyToManyField` directly, but often, you'll want to track extra data on the relationship itself—like when the student enrolled or their progress. To do that, you define an explicit intermediary model.

```python
class Student(models.Model):
    full_name = models.CharField(max_length=150)
    email = models.EmailField(unique=True)
    registered_at =
models.DateTimeField(auto_now_add=True)

    def __str__(self):
```

```
        return self.full_name

class Enrollment(models.Model):
    student = models.ForeignKey(Student,
on_delete=models.CASCADE,
related_name='enrollments')
    course = models.ForeignKey(Course,
on_delete=models.CASCADE,
related_name='enrollments')
    enrolled_on =
models.DateTimeField(auto_now_add=True)
    progress = models.DecimalField(max_digits=5,
decimal_places=2, default=0.0)

    class Meta:
        unique_together = ('student', 'course')

    def __str__(self):
        return f"{self.student.full_name} in
{self.course.title}"
```

With this setup, you have complete control over the relationship. You can prevent duplicates with the `unique_together` constraint. This ensures a student can't enroll in the same course more than once, even if you forget to check manually in your code.

To retrieve all the students enrolled in a given course:

```
course = Course.objects.get(id=1)
students =
Student.objects.filter(enrollments__course=course)
```

And to get all the courses a student is enrolled in:

```
student = Student.objects.get(id=1)
courses =
Course.objects.filter(enrollments__student=student)
```

These queries leverage the `related_name` properties on the `ForeignKey` fields, which keep your ORM usage clean and expressive.

Now let's talk about **constraints**. Constraints are rules that the database enforces to ensure data integrity. You've already seen `unique_together`, which prevents duplicate combinations. Django 3.2+ introduced `UniqueConstraint` with more flexibility:

```
class Enrollment(models.Model):
    ...
    class Meta:
        constraints = [

models.UniqueConstraint(fields=['student',
'course'], name='unique_enrollment')
        ]
```

This does the same thing, but with a named constraint. Naming your constraints makes debugging easier, especially when your app grows and you have many models interacting with each other.

You can also use other constraints to enforce business rules. For example, maybe students can't have progress over 100%. You could enforce that with a model-level validator:

```
from django.core.exceptions import ValidationError

class Enrollment(models.Model):
    ...
    def clean(self):
        if self.progress > 100:
            raise ValidationError("Progress cannot
exceed 100%")
```

This validation runs when you call `.full_clean()` or use Django forms or serializers that handle validation. It won't automatically run on `save()` unless you explicitly call it, so keep that in mind. When using Django REST Framework, these model-level validations can be integrated into your serializers.

Another useful constraint is `CheckConstraint`, which ensures that numeric fields remain within valid ranges:

```
class Meta:
    constraints = [
        models.CheckConstraint(
```

```
            check=models.Q(progress__gte=0) &
models.Q(progress__lte=100),
            name='valid_progress_range'
        )
    ]
```

This protects your database from invalid values, even if your application code forgets to validate them.

Finally, let's consider **nullability** and **blank values**. These two flags work differently in Django.

`null=True` means the field can be `NULL` in the database.

`blank=True` means the field can be left empty in forms or serializers.

If you want a field to be optional in both the database and the user interface, set both `null=True` and `blank=True`. This distinction matters when you're building APIs and want certain fields to be required or optional.

For example:

```
class Course(models.Model):
    description = models.TextField(blank=True,
null=True)
```

This means `description` can be left out of the API payload, and the database will store a `NULL` instead of an empty string.

Clean relationships and constraints keep your data safe and your logic consistent. When you model relationships carefully, you prevent bad data from entering the system and reduce the complexity of your business logic. Instead of checking for duplicates in your view, the database enforces it for you. Instead of manually rejecting a student's second enrollment, the `UniqueConstraint` does it with a single rule.

These design decisions don't just affect your models—they directly influence how you write your serializers, your views, and your tests. That's why the time you spend defining clear relationships and applying appropriate constraints will save you hours later on.

Writing Clean, Maintainable Models

When you're building the backend of an application—especially an API-first one—your models define the structure and behavior of your data. They don't just represent database tables. They reflect business logic, relationships, and rules that make up the core of your system.

So the way you write your models matters. Clean models are easy to read, test, and extend. They behave predictably. And most importantly, they make your entire project easier to work with—not just for you, but for every developer who comes after you.

Let's walk through how to write models that are not only correct, but clear and maintainable.

Start by focusing on **naming**. Field names should be unambiguous, lowercase, and descriptive without being redundant. A `User` model shouldn't have a field called `user_email`. Just call it `email`. If a field represents a relationship, make sure its name is easy to understand in both directions.

Here's an example:

```
class Instructor(models.Model):
    full_name = models.CharField(max_length=150)
    email = models.EmailField(unique=True)
    bio = models.TextField(blank=True)
```

This model is clear. Each field name tells you what it represents. There's no confusion about what data each field holds, and there are no unnecessary abbreviations or acronyms. You could hand this to someone who's never seen the code and they'd understand what it does in seconds.

Next, use the correct **field types**. Django gives you a rich set of fields to describe your data accurately. Use `EmailField` for email addresses. Use `DateTimeField` for timestamps. Don't fall into the trap of using `CharField` for everything just because it feels easier.

bFor example, if you have a boolean flag, use `BooleanField`, not a string that says `"yes"` or `"no"`.

```
class Course(models.Model):
    ...
    is_published =
models.BooleanField(default=False)
```

This lets you filter with expressive queries like:

```
Course.objects.filter(is_published=True)
```

Now let's talk about **defaults and nullability**. If a field must always have a value, don't make it nullable. If it's optional, make sure that's reflected in both the database and your serializers or forms.

Here's how you could handle optional fields:

```
class Course(models.Model):
    description = models.TextField(blank=True,
null=True)
```

This field can be omitted from forms and stored as NULL in the database. If it's only optional for the UI but should never be null in the database, use:

```
class Course(models.Model):
    description = models.TextField(blank=True)
```

This enforces the difference between "empty string" and "no value at all."

A clean model should also have a clear string representation. That means always implement __str__():

```
class Course(models.Model):
    title = models.CharField(max_length=255)
    ...

    def __str__(self):
        return self.title
```

This helps with debugging, admin display, and logs. Without it, you'll see cryptic entries like `Course object (3)` instead of something useful like `Python Fundamentals`.

If your model has logic that's specific to how it behaves, put that logic **in the model**. Don't spread it out across views or serializers if it belongs close to the

63

data. For example, if you want to check whether a course is active based on the publish date and a flag:

```
class Course(models.Model):
    ...
    publish_date = models.DateField()
    is_published =
models.BooleanField(default=False)

    def is_active(self):
        from django.utils.timezone import now
        return self.is_published and
self.publish_date <= now().date()
```

Now you can write clear, readable logic elsewhere in your code:

```
if course.is_active():

    show_to_students(course)
```

This is better than duplicating the condition in every view or API method. You've centralized the business rule where it belongs.

You can take this further by writing **custom model managers** to encapsulate reusable query logic.

```
class CourseQuerySet(models.QuerySet):
    def published(self):
        return self.filter(is_published=True)

    def active(self):
        from django.utils.timezone import now
        return self.filter(is_published=True,
publish_date__lte=now().date())

class Course(models.Model):
    ...
    objects = CourseQuerySet.as_manager()
```

Now your code becomes more expressive:

```
Course.objects.active()
Course.objects.published()
```

This keeps queries consistent, reduces duplication, and makes your intent clear every time you query the model.

You should also think about **indexes and constraints** early. If a field will be queried frequently—like `email` or `slug`—it should be indexed or unique:

```
email = models.EmailField(unique=True)
slug = models.SlugField(max_length=100,
unique=True)
```

Django automatically creates indexes for fields with `unique=True`. For performance-critical queries that aren't unique, you can add a custom index:

```
class Meta:
    indexes = [
        models.Index(fields=['is_published',
'publish_date']),
    ]
```

This improves query performance and prepares your model for growth.

You'll also want to organize your models in a way that scales. That means splitting them across apps when they serve different parts of your project. A large monolithic `models.py` file becomes hard to navigate as your app grows. Create separate apps like `courses`, `accounts`, and `payments`, and define models in those apps.

For example:

```
courses/
    models.py   # Course, Instructor, Enrollment
accounts/
    models.py   # Student, UserProfile
payments/
    models.py   # Transaction, Invoice
```

This keeps your codebase modular and makes it easier to test and maintain.

And finally, write **docstrings** or comments where necessary—not everywhere, but where it helps someone understand why a field or method exists.

```
class Enrollment(models.Model):
    ...
```

```
    # Tracks a student's progress as a percentage
(0 to 100)
    progress = models.DecimalField(max_digits=5,
decimal_places=2, default=0.0)
```

This tells the next developer—or your future self—how to interpret that field, without needing to trace it through business logic.

Clean models are not just about passing migrations. They're about writing code that makes your intentions obvious. Code that tells the truth about the data it represents. And code that supports your entire application, from database to API, in a way that's easy to reason about, easy to change, and easy to trust.

A well-written model becomes the most stable and reliable part of your application. That's what you want at the heart of your data layer.

Initial Migrations and Data Seeding

After you've defined your models, Django needs to know how to translate those Python classes into actual database tables. That's what migrations are for. Migrations are Django's way of tracking changes to your models over time and applying those changes to your database in a structured, version-controlled way.

When you define a model, it doesn't affect the database immediately. Django holds onto the model structure until you explicitly generate a migration. This is an important safety feature—it ensures that your database is always updated intentionally and traceably.

Let's say you've written this model in core/models.py:

```
from django.db import models

class Instructor(models.Model):
    full_name = models.CharField(max_length=150)
    email = models.EmailField(unique=True)
    bio = models.TextField(blank=True)

    def __str__(self):
```

```
        return self.full_name
```

Once this model is in place, the first step is to generate the initial migration file.

Run this in your terminal:

```
python manage.py makemigrations
```

Django will scan your installed apps, detect any changes to the models, and create a new file in `core/migrations/`. The file will have a name like `0001_initial.py`. It contains the instructions for creating the `Instructor` table in SQL, but written in Python using Django's migration framework.

Next, you apply the migration:

```
python manage.py migrate
```

This executes the SQL needed to create the actual database table. At this point, the table for `Instructor` now exists in your database and is ready to store real data.

The migration system also creates a special table called `django_migrations` to keep track of which migrations have been applied. This way, Django knows what's already been executed and won't repeat the same operation.

Once your models are migrated, you may want to **seed the database with initial data**—records that help with testing, development, or even production bootstrapping. Django gives you a few options for this.

One method is to use **fixtures**. A fixture is a file—usually in JSON or YAML format—that contains serialized objects. You load it with a simple command.

Here's what a fixture might look like for instructors:

```
[
  {
    "model": "core.instructor",
    "pk": 1,
    "fields": {
      "full_name": "Jane Doe",
      "email": "jane@example.com",
```

```
      "bio": "Senior backend instructor with 10
years of experience."
    }
  },
  {
    "model": "core.instructor",
    "pk": 2,
    "fields": {
      "full_name": "John Smith",
      "email": "john@example.com",
      "bio": "Expert in Django and REST APIs."
    }
  }
]
```

Save this as `core/fixtures/instructors.json`, then load it into your database like this:

```
python manage.py loaddata core/fixtures/instructors.json
```

Django will create those two instructor records, preserving the primary keys if possible. Fixtures are helpful when you want portable seed data that can be checked into version control and reused across environments.

Another approach is to use **custom management commands** or a **data seeding script**.

Let's say you want to programmatically generate 50 fake instructors for development and testing. You can use Python's `Faker` library and write a management command like this:

First, install Faker if you haven't already:

```
pip install faker
```

Then create the command:

```
# core/management/commands/seed_instructors.py

from django.core.management.base import BaseCommand
from core.models import Instructor
from faker import Faker

class Command(BaseCommand):
```

```
    help = 'Seed the database with fake instructor
data'

    def handle(self, *args, **kwargs):
        fake = Faker()
        for _ in range(50):
            Instructor.objects.create(
                full_name=fake.name(),
                email=fake.unique.email(),
                bio=fake.text(max_nb_chars=200)
            )

self.stdout.write(self.style.SUCCESS('Successfully
seeded 50 instructors.'))
```

Now run the command:

```
python manage.py seed_instructors
```

This is especially useful for creating larger datasets that you don't want to hand-write. It also helps simulate real-world usage and makes your API feel more realistic during frontend or client development.

If you're using **Docker** or automated deployment scripts, you can call your seed command as part of the setup pipeline. That way, every new environment gets initialized with meaningful starter data.

You can also mix seeding with conditional logic. For example, if you only want to seed data in development environments:

```
import os

if os.environ.get('DJANGO_ENV') == 'development':
    # seed data
```

This helps you avoid accidentally populating production databases with test data.

Another place where initial data matters is in creating essential users, such as superusers or API clients. You can do this directly inside `manage.py shell`, or automate it with a one-time script like this:

```
from django.contrib.auth import get_user_model
```

```
User = get_user_model()
if not
User.objects.filter(email='admin@example.com').exis
ts():

User.objects.create_superuser('admin@example.com',
'adminpass')
```

This logic can live inside a startup hook, a deployment script, or a one-off data migration.

To summarize this workflow in practice:

You define your models in `models.py`.

You run `makemigrations` to generate a migration file.

You run `migrate` to apply it and update the database schema.

You load initial data using `loaddata`, a custom command, or by scripting it directly.

This process ensures your database evolves safely and reproducibly across environments—local development, staging, and production. And it gives your team a predictable way to bootstrap data for testing, demo, or integration purposes.

Integrating Model Logic into API Design

The structure and behavior of your models directly influence the usability, clarity, and efficiency of your API. When your models encapsulate logic thoughtfully, your views, serializers, and endpoints become cleaner and more consistent. Instead of spreading business rules across the API layer, you anchor them where they belong: in the data layer, where they can be reused, tested, and maintained with confidence.

Your API is an interface to your domain logic. And the more your models express that logic clearly, the more your API can behave like a true representation of the business problem it's solving.

Start with a clear model that does more than just store data. Let's say you're building a course enrollment system. You already have a model like this:

```python
# courses/models.py

from django.db import models
from django.utils.timezone import now

class Course(models.Model):
    title = models.CharField(max_length=255)
    description = models.TextField()
    publish_date = models.DateField()
    is_published =
models.BooleanField(default=False)

    def __str__(self):
        return self.title

    def is_active(self):
        return self.is_published and
self.publish_date <= now().date()
```

That `is_active()` method reflects a simple piece of logic: a course should only be considered active if it's marked as published and the publish date has arrived.

Rather than duplicating that logic in your views or serializers, you keep it in the model. Now your API code can call this method with confidence, whether you're writing a filter, a computed field, or a condition in a custom permission class.

Let's expose this logic in your API response.

In your `CourseSerializer`, include a read-only field:

```python
# courses/serializers.py

from rest_framework import serializers
from .models import Course

class
CourseSerializer(serializers.ModelSerializer):
    is_active = serializers.SerializerMethodField()
```

```python
    class Meta:
        model = Course
        fields = ['id', 'title', 'description',
'publish_date', 'is_published', 'is_active']

    def get_is_active(self, obj):
        return obj.is_active()
```

Now every time a client fetches a course object, they get a field that tells them whether the course is active—without needing to reconstruct that logic themselves. The behavior is encapsulated in the model, and the API simply reflects it.

This is how you build expressive APIs: not by pushing logic into serializers, but by letting the model define how it behaves.

You can apply this principle to computed properties, formatting methods, custom queryset filters, and validation rules.

Let's go deeper with a more advanced example. Say you want to allow instructors to enroll students in courses, but only if the course is active. Instead of putting that logic in your view or serializer, you can enforce it in the model:

```python
# courses/models.py

class Enrollment(models.Model):
    student = models.ForeignKey('accounts.Student',
on_delete=models.CASCADE)
    course = models.ForeignKey(Course,
on_delete=models.CASCADE)
    enrolled_on =
models.DateTimeField(auto_now_add=True)

    def clean(self):
        if not self.course.is_active():
            from django.core.exceptions import
ValidationError
            raise ValidationError("Cannot enroll in
a course that is not active.")
```

This logic will be triggered automatically if you call `.full_clean()` on the model. DRF's `ModelSerializer` handles this for you behind the scenes when validating data during `create()` and `update()`.

Here's how the corresponding serializer might look:

```python
# courses/serializers.py

from rest_framework import serializers
from .models import Enrollment

class
EnrollmentSerializer(serializers.ModelSerializer):
    class Meta:
        model = Enrollment
        fields = '__all__'
```

You don't need to duplicate any logic in the serializer. The model enforces its rules, and DRF will automatically raise a validation error if the business condition fails. The response might look like this:

```json
{
  "non_field_errors": ["Cannot enroll in a course
that is not active."]
}
```

This behavior is consistent, reusable, and easy to test.

Now let's look at filtering data based on model logic. Suppose you want to create an endpoint that lists only the active courses.

Rather than writing a hardcoded filter every time, define a custom queryset on your model:

```python
class CourseQuerySet(models.QuerySet):
    def active(self):
        from django.utils.timezone import now
        return self.filter(is_published=True,
publish_date__lte=now().date())

class Course(models.Model):
    ...
    objects = CourseQuerySet.as_manager()
```

Then in your view:

```python
# courses/views.py

from rest_framework import viewsets
from .models import Course
from .serializers import CourseSerializer

class
ActiveCourseViewSet(viewsets.ReadOnlyModelViewSet):
    queryset = Course.objects.active()
    serializer_class = CourseSerializer
```

By moving the logic into the model's custom manager, you make the filtering logic reusable. You could apply the same logic to reports, background jobs, or dashboard views without repeating yourself.

You can also use this approach to simplify complex queries. For example:

```python
class CourseQuerySet(models.QuerySet):
    def upcoming(self):
        return
self.filter(publish_date__gt=now().date())

    def empty(self):
        return
self.annotate(enrollment_count=models.Count('enroll
ment')).filter(enrollment_count=0)
```

Then in your views or filters:

```python
Course.objects.upcoming()
Course.objects.empty()
```

Another place where model logic improves API design is in custom actions.

Let's say you want to expose an API endpoint that lets instructors close enrollment for a course. That action has to change the state of the course—but it should also respect business rules, like not closing enrollment for a course that hasn't been published.

You can define the method on the model:

```python
class Course(models.Model):
```

```
    . . .
    enrollment_closed =
models.BooleanField(default=False)

    def close_enrollment(self):
        if not self.is_published:
            raise ValueError("Cannot close
enrollment on an unpublished course.")
        self.enrollment_closed = True
        self.save()
```

Then use a DRF viewset action to expose it:

```
# courses/views.py

from rest_framework.decorators import action
from rest_framework.response import Response
from rest_framework import status

class CourseViewSet(viewsets.ModelViewSet):
    queryset = Course.objects.all()
    serializer_class = CourseSerializer

    @action(detail=True, methods=['post'])
    def close_enrollment(self, request, pk=None):
        course = self.get_object()
        try:
            course.close_enrollment()
            return Response({'message': 'Enrollment
closed successfully.'})
        except ValueError as e:
            return Response({'error': str(e)},
status=status.HTTP_400_BAD_REQUEST)
```

This pattern keeps the model in charge of business logic and the API responsible for user interaction. The result is a predictable, clean interface that enforces the same rules no matter where the method is used.

When you integrate logic into your models, you're giving your API a reliable contract. You're saying: "This is how this data behaves—everywhere." And you're reducing the risk of bugs, duplicated conditions, and drift between layers of your application.

Your API becomes easier to maintain because your business rules live close to the data they affect. You can test them directly using Django's test framework without needing to go through serializers or views. And when the rules change, you only have to update them in one place.

This isn't just a best practice. It's one of the most effective ways to build APIs that stay clean and manageable over time.

Chapter 4: Serializers and Views in Depth

When you're building a Django REST API, two layers matter just as much as your models: your **serializers** and your **views**. These are the parts of your application that handle incoming data from the client and send back structured responses. Your models define what your system is. Your serializers and views define how others interact with it.

In this chapter, we'll take a complete look at both. You'll learn how to structure your serializers, validate user input, write clean views, reuse logic across endpoints, and customize how your API responds to different scenarios. Each concept is grounded in real-world patterns and built around Django REST Framework's idiomatic style.

Serializers and Model Serializers

In Django REST Framework, serializers are responsible for converting complex data types—like Django model instances—into native Python datatypes that can then be rendered into JSON, XML, or other formats. They also handle deserialization: validating and converting incoming data back into complex Python objects.

This conversion process is a crucial part of any API, because it determines how your data is structured, validated, and communicated to external clients. When designed carefully, serializers make your API predictable, secure, and easy to consume.

Let's take a real-world example. You're building an API for an online learning platform, and you have a model called `Course`.

```python
# courses/models.py

from django.db import models

class Course(models.Model):
    title = models.CharField(max_length=255)
    description = models.TextField()
```

```
    publish_date = models.DateField()
    is_published =
models.BooleanField(default=False)

    def __str__(self):
        return self.title
```

Now, you need a way to expose this model through your API—both for reading data (serialization) and for accepting new data from users (deserialization).

You can start with a basic serializer by explicitly defining each field:

```
# courses/serializers.py

from rest_framework import serializers
from .models import Course

class CourseSerializer(serializers.Serializer):
    id = serializers.IntegerField(read_only=True)
    title = serializers.CharField(max_length=255)
    description = serializers.CharField()
    publish_date = serializers.DateField()
    is_published = serializers.BooleanField()
```

This serializer defines how the Course model is translated to and from JSON. The id field is marked as read-only because it's assigned automatically by the database. All the other fields match what you defined in the model.

You can use this serializer in a view to create new courses or return a list of existing ones. But you'll quickly find that manually managing each field becomes tedious, especially when working with many models or large models. This is where ModelSerializer becomes extremely useful.

A ModelSerializer automatically generates a set of fields based on the model definition. Here's how you can use it to simplify the previous serializer:

```
class
CourseSerializer(serializers.ModelSerializer):
    class Meta:
        model = Course
        fields = '__all__'
```

The `fields = '__all__'` line tells DRF to include all model fields in the serializer. You can also specify a subset, like `fields = ['id', 'title', 'is_published']`, if you want to limit the exposed data.

Using `ModelSerializer` doesn't mean you're giving up control. You can still override individual field behavior, add extra fields, and define validation logic.

For example, say you want to add a custom read-only field called `status`, which reflects whether the course is upcoming, active, or archived:

```
class
CourseSerializer(serializers.ModelSerializer):
    status = serializers.SerializerMethodField()

    class Meta:
        model = Course
        fields = ['id', 'title', 'description',
'publish_date', 'is_published', 'status']

    def get_status(self, obj):
        from django.utils.timezone import now
        today = now().date()
        if not obj.is_published:
            return 'Draft'
        elif obj.publish_date > today:
            return 'Upcoming'
        else:
            return 'Active'
```

This pattern is especially useful when you want to expose computed fields that don't exist in your model but still belong in the API response.

Let's look at another common scenario: nested relationships.

Suppose you have a related model `Instructor`:

```
class Instructor(models.Model):
    name = models.CharField(max_length=100)
    bio = models.TextField()
```

And your `Course` model has a foreign key:

```
class Course(models.Model):
```

```
...
    instructor = models.ForeignKey(Instructor,
on_delete=models.CASCADE, related_name='courses')
```

If you want to include the instructor's name in the course response, you have a few options.

To show just the name, without nesting:

```
class
CourseSerializer(serializers.ModelSerializer):
    instructor_name =
serializers.CharField(source='instructor.name',
read_only=True)

    class Meta:
        model = Course
        fields = ['id', 'title', 'instructor_name']
```

If you want to include full instructor data in a nested format, define another serializer:

```
class
InstructorSerializer(serializers.ModelSerializer):
    class Meta:
        model = Instructor
        fields = ['id', 'name', 'bio']

class
CourseSerializer(serializers.ModelSerializer):
    instructor =
InstructorSerializer(read_only=True)

    class Meta:
        model = Course
        fields = ['id', 'title', 'instructor']
```

This gives clients a complete JSON structure with related data:

```
{
  "id": 3,
  "title": "Advanced Python",
  "instructor": {
```

```
      "id": 1,
      "name": "Jane Doe",
      "bio": "Senior Python developer."
   }
}
```

If you want to allow clients to assign an instructor by ID during creation, you can combine both approaches using `PrimaryKeyRelatedField` for writes and a nested serializer for reads:

```
class
CourseSerializer(serializers.ModelSerializer):
    instructor =
serializers.PrimaryKeyRelatedField(queryset=Instruc
tor.objects.all())
    instructor_details =
InstructorSerializer(source='instructor',
read_only=True)

    class Meta:
        model = Course
        fields = ['id', 'title', 'instructor',
'instructor_details']
```

With this setup, clients send only the instructor ID when creating or updating a course:

```
{
  "title": "Intro to Django",
  "instructor": 2
}
```

But they still get the full instructor information in the response.

Working with serializers also gives you control over field visibility. You can make fields read-only, write-only, or hidden.

If you want to track the user who created a course but don't want clients to provide that field explicitly:

```
class
CourseSerializer(serializers.ModelSerializer):
    class Meta:
```

```
        model = Course
        fields = '__all__'
        read_only_fields = ['created_by']

    def create(self, validated_data):
        validated_data['created_by'] =
self.context['request'].user
        return super().create(validated_data)
```
Now, `created_by` is automatically set based on the authenticated user, and clients can't modify it.

The `context['request']` object is available inside serializers when they're used in views. It's a powerful way to pass additional data into the serialization process.

In short, serializers aren't just data translators. They are central to your API's behavior. They define which data is exposed, how it's validated, and how it's transformed. A well-structured serializer clarifies the contract between your API and its clients. And using `ModelSerializer` gives you all the power of DRF's validation, while keeping your code concise and maintainable.

As your models evolve, your serializers help you keep your API responses consistent. And when you want to introduce custom logic—computed fields, nested data, or business rules—serializers give you the hooks to do it cleanly.

Validation Strategies and Custom Serializer Fields

When a client sends data to your API—whether it's creating a new user, submitting a form, or updating a record—you can't assume that the data is valid, complete, or even safe. It's your job to validate that data before it reaches your models. This is one of the core responsibilities of serializers in Django REST Framework.

Validation isn't just about making sure a field isn't blank or that a string is the right length. It's about enforcing business rules, protecting data integrity, and communicating clear error messages when something goes wrong. In this section, you'll learn exactly how to do that—cleanly and effectively—using DRF's validation system and custom serializer fields.

If you've defined a `ModelSerializer`, Django REST Framework already applies the model-level field validations. For example, if your model includes `blank=False`, `max_length=255`, or `unique=True`, those rules are automatically enforced.

Here's a model you might be working with:

```python
# courses/models.py

from django.db import models

class Course(models.Model):
    title = models.CharField(max_length=100)
    description = models.TextField(blank=True)
    is_published =
models.BooleanField(default=False)
    publish_date = models.DateField(null=True,
blank=True)
```

Now define a serializer:

```python
# courses/serializers.py

from rest_framework import serializers
from .models import Course

class
CourseSerializer(serializers.ModelSerializer):
    class Meta:
        model = Course
        fields = '__all__'
```

At this point, DRF automatically ensures that `title` is present and under 100 characters, and that `is_published` is a boolean. But what about a rule that says, "If a course is published, then a publish date is required"?

That's not something the model handles directly. It's a **cross-field validation**, and you can enforce it with the `validate()` method:

83

```
class
CourseSerializer(serializers.ModelSerializer):
    class Meta:
        model = Course
        fields = '__all__'

    def validate(self, data):
        if data.get('is_published') and not
data.get('publish_date'):
            raise serializers.ValidationError({
                'publish_date': 'Publish date is
required when the course is marked as published.'
            })
        return data
```

This method runs after all individual fields are validated, and before the create() or update() methods are called. If the validation fails, DRF returns a 400 response with your message.

Now let's look at **field-level validation**. Suppose you want to reject titles that consist only of whitespace. That's a per-field check, and it belongs in validate_<fieldname>():

```
    def validate_title(self, value):
        if not value.strip():
            raise
serializers.ValidationError("Title cannot be
blank.")
        return value
```

Each of these methods should return the cleaned value. If they raise an error, that error will be attached to the relevant field in the response.

Next, let's talk about custom fields—fields that don't exist in your model, but are calculated or formatted specifically for the API.

Start with a read-only computed field. Let's say you want to include a status in the response, based on the is_published flag and the publish date.

```
    status = serializers.SerializerMethodField()

    def get_status(self, obj):
        from django.utils.timezone import now
```

```
        today = now().date()
        if not obj.is_published:
            return "Draft"
        elif obj.publish_date and obj.publish_date
> today:
            return "Scheduled"
        else:
            return "Live"
```

This `status` field is not in your model, but it gives your frontend team clear insight into how the course should be displayed. `SerializerMethodField` is read-only by default, so you don't need to validate it.

Now let's say you want to accept a custom input field, like `duration_in_weeks`, which doesn't exist in your model but is used to compute other values. You can add it as a regular field and then consume it in your `create()` or `update()` methods.

Here's how you might do that:

```
class
CourseSerializer(serializers.ModelSerializer):
    duration_in_weeks =
serializers.IntegerField(write_only=True,
required=False)

    class Meta:
        model = Course
        fields = ['id', 'title', 'description',
'is_published', 'publish_date',
'duration_in_weeks']

    def create(self, validated_data):
        duration =
validated_data.pop('duration_in_weeks', None)
        # You can use `duration` here to influence
other logic
        course =
Course.objects.create(**validated_data)
        return course
```

With `write_only=True`, this field is accepted in the input but never shown in the API response. That's useful for form-like behavior where a temporary input value triggers a side effect.

Another advanced use case is dynamically controlling field behavior based on context. Suppose admin users are allowed to publish courses, but regular users are not. You can override the serializer's `__init__` method to conditionally make `is_published` read-only:

```
def __init__(self, *args, **kwargs):
    super().__init__(*args, **kwargs)
    user = self.context['request'].user
    if not user.is_staff:
        self.fields['is_published'].read_only = True
```

This pattern gives you precise control over what users can or cannot edit, without having to split your serializers into multiple classes.

You can also add **custom validators** that apply to a field across different serializers.

Let's say you want to enforce a rule across multiple models: titles should never contain the word "free". You can define a reusable validator function:

```
from rest_framework import serializers

def no_banned_words(value):
    if 'free' in value.lower():
        raise serializers.ValidationError("Titles
cannot contain the word 'free'.")
    return value
```

Then apply it to any field:

```
title =
serializers.CharField(validators=[no_banned_words])
```

This keeps your logic clean and encourages reuse across your serializers.

In cases where validation fails, the client receives a clear JSON structure like:

```
{
```

```
  "title": ["Titles cannot contain the word
'free'"],
  "publish_date": ["Publish date is required when
the course is marked as published."]
}
```

This format is predictable, easy to parse on the frontend, and informative for users.

If you want to override the structure of validation errors—for example, wrapping all errors inside a `"errors"` key—you can override the view's exception handler. But for most use cases, DRF's built-in formatting is both conventional and practical.

Validation is about more than data correctness. It's a way to protect your application's business logic, prevent developer mistakes, and provide clear feedback to API consumers. The goal is not just to block bad data—but to explain why the data is invalid and what the client should do differently.

As your application grows, you'll encounter more complex validation needs—across relationships, permissions, or external systems. The techniques you've learned here—field-level methods, cross-field logic, dynamic behavior, custom validators, and context-aware rules—will carry you through those challenges with clarity and confidence.

APIViews, Generic Views, and ViewSets

In Django REST Framework, the way you structure your views has a direct impact on how maintainable, testable, and expressive your API becomes. Views are responsible for handling incoming requests, running the necessary logic, and returning a structured response. DRF gives you multiple ways to implement views, and the right choice often depends on how much control you need and how much boilerplate you're willing to manage.

The three primary approaches are:

APIView, where you write each HTTP method explicitly

Generic class-based views, which provide common patterns out of the box

ViewSets, which group related actions into a single class and are typically paired with DRF's routers

Using APIView for Full Control

`APIView` is DRF's base class for building views that respond to HTTP methods like GET, POST, PUT, and DELETE. When you use this class, you implement each method yourself, giving you complete control over the logic.

This is useful when your behavior doesn't fit the standard CRUD model, or when you need to handle request data in a non-standard way.

Here's a simple example:

```python
# courses/views.py

from rest_framework.views import APIView
from rest_framework.response import Response
from rest_framework import status
from .models import Course
from .serializers import CourseSerializer

class CourseListCreateView(APIView):
    def get(self, request):
        courses = Course.objects.all()
        serializer = CourseSerializer(courses,
many=True)
        return Response(serializer.data)

    def post(self, request):
        serializer =
CourseSerializer(data=request.data)
        if serializer.is_valid():
            serializer.save()
            return Response(serializer.data,
status=status.HTTP_201_CREATED)
        return Response(serializer.errors,
status=status.HTTP_400_BAD_REQUEST)
```

Each method receives the request and returns a `Response` object. This gives you fine-grained control over what happens before and after serialization, including custom authentication, permission checks, or transformations.

If you need a detailed endpoint where each method behaves differently, `APIView` is a good starting point. But it does require you to manage common patterns like queryset handling and serializer setup yourself.

Using Generic Views for Reusable CRUD Behavior

Django REST Framework includes a set of **generic views** that cover the most common use cases, such as listing data, creating objects, retrieving a single instance, updating, or deleting.

These views automatically handle much of the boilerplate you'd otherwise write yourself with `APIView`. You just need to define two things:

`queryset`: the set of objects this view works with

`serializer_class`: the serializer used for reading and writing data

Here's the same functionality from above using `ListCreateAPIView`:

```
from rest_framework.generics import
ListCreateAPIView
from .models import Course
from .serializers import CourseSerializer

class CourseListCreateView(ListCreateAPIView):
    queryset = Course.objects.all()
    serializer_class = CourseSerializer
```

DRF handles everything: querying the data, paginating the results, validating input, saving new objects, and formatting the output.

To retrieve, update, or delete a single course, you'd use another generic view:

```
from rest_framework.generics import
RetrieveUpdateDestroyAPIView

class
CourseDetailView(RetrieveUpdateDestroyAPIView):
    queryset = Course.objects.all()
    serializer_class = CourseSerializer
```

Generic views are ideal when you're following typical CRUD patterns and don't need to customize every part of the workflow. They also make testing and refactoring much easier because each class has a clear, focused purpose.

If you need a custom permission, filter, or response format, you can still override methods like `get_queryset()`, `perform_create()`, or `get_serializer_context()` without losing the benefits of the abstraction.

Using ViewSets for Unified Endpoints

`ViewSets` go one step further and allow you to define all related operations (list, retrieve, create, update, delete) in a single class. Unlike generic views, which map one class per endpoint, viewsets are meant to be connected to URLs using a **router**.

This keeps your code organized and consistent, especially for large APIs.

Here's a full-featured example:

```python
from rest_framework import viewsets
from .models import Course
from .serializers import CourseSerializer

class CourseViewSet(viewsets.ModelViewSet):
    queryset = Course.objects.all()
    serializer_class = CourseSerializer
```

This single class supports all of the following actions:

GET `/courses/` → list

POST `/courses/` → create

GET `/courses/<id>/` → retrieve

PUT `/courses/<id>/` → update

PATCH `/courses/<id>/` → partial update

DELETE `/courses/<id>/` → destroy

To make this work, you register the viewset in your router:

```python
from rest_framework.routers import DefaultRouter
```

```
from .views import CourseViewSet

router = DefaultRouter()
router.register(r'courses', CourseViewSet)

urlpatterns = [
    path('api/', include(router.urls)),
]
```

If you only want certain actions (for example, list and retrieve), use `ReadOnlyModelViewSet`:

```
from rest_framework.viewsets import
ReadOnlyModelViewSet

class PublicCourseViewSet(ReadOnlyModelViewSet):
    queryset =
Course.objects.filter(is_published=True)
    serializer_class = CourseSerializer
```

You can also write **custom actions** with `@action` decorators:

```
from rest_framework.decorators import action
from rest_framework.response import Response

class CourseViewSet(viewsets.ModelViewSet):
    ...

    @action(detail=True, methods=['post'])
    def close_enrollment(self, request, pk=None):
        course = self.get_object()
        course.is_published = False
        course.save()
        return Response({'status': 'enrollment
closed'})
```

This gives you a flexible API without losing structure.

Use `APIView` when you need complete control over request handling and you're not following standard patterns. For example, if you're writing an endpoint that aggregates data, runs custom authentication, or interacts with external APIs.

Use generic views when your endpoint fits the standard CRUD operations and you want to keep your code concise and readable.

Use viewsets when you want a clean, unified class for all operations on a resource, especially when paired with DRF routers to generate URLs automatically.

All three approaches are valid and fully supported. The key is to be consistent, and to choose the level of abstraction that matches the complexity of your logic.

In most real-world APIs, you'll end up using a mix. Generic views for common endpoints. APIView for special cases. And viewsets for large, well-defined resources like `users`, `courses`, or `products`.

Whichever one you choose, the structure of your views has a direct impact on how quickly others can understand your API, how easy it is to extend, and how well it aligns with your serializers and models.

In the next section, we'll look at how to build reusable view logic using mixins—so you don't have to duplicate behavior across multiple classes, and can build just the functionality you need. But now you have a solid foundation for structuring your API endpoints using Django REST Framework's most important view patterns.

Building Reusable View Logic with Mixins

When you're building APIs, not every view needs the full CRUD functionality that a `ModelViewSet` provides. Sometimes, you only need a read-only endpoint. Sometimes you want to allow updates but not deletes. Django REST Framework gives you the flexibility to construct exactly what you need through **mixins**—modular, reusable building blocks for view logic.

Mixins are especially useful when your views follow conventional patterns (like create, retrieve, list, update, or delete), but you want full control over which capabilities to include. Using mixins helps you avoid rewriting common logic and gives you more flexibility than generic views or viewsets alone.

Starting with a Practical Scenario

Suppose you're building an API for a public course catalog. Users can browse the courses and read the details, but they aren't allowed to modify anything.

You don't need create, update, or delete views—only list and retrieve.

You can compose that behavior using `ListModelMixin` and `RetrieveModelMixin`, along with `GenericAPIView`.

Here's how that looks:

```python
# courses/views.py

from rest_framework import mixins, generics
from .models import Course
from .serializers import CourseSerializer

class PublicCourseView(mixins.ListModelMixin,
                       mixins.RetrieveModelMixin,
                       generics.GenericAPIView):
    queryset =
Course.objects.filter(is_published=True)
    serializer_class = CourseSerializer

    def get(self, request, *args, **kwargs):
        if 'pk' in kwargs:
            return self.retrieve(request, *args,
**kwargs)
        return self.list(request, *args, **kwargs)
```

This view supports two routes:

`GET /api/courses/` — list all published courses

`GET /api/courses/<id>/` — get a specific course

By combining the mixins with `GenericAPIView`, you keep full control over method dispatch, queryset filtering, and response formatting, but you don't have to write your own pagination, serialization, or error handling. The mixins do that for you.

How Mixins Work

Each mixin implements just one HTTP method. Here's what they do:

`ListModelMixin` provides `.list()`, used for GET requests on a collection

`RetrieveModelMixin` provides `.retrieve()`, used for GET requests on a single object

`CreateModelMixin` provides `.create()`, used for POST requests

`UpdateModelMixin` provides `.update()`, used for PUT and PATCH

`DestroyModelMixin` provides `.destroy()`, used for DELETE

You can include only the ones you need. For example, let's say you want to allow authenticated users to **submit new course suggestions**, but you don't want to expose any update or delete functionality.

Here's the view:

```
from rest_framework import mixins, generics
from .models import Course
from .serializers import CourseSerializer
from rest_framework.permissions import
IsAuthenticated

class CourseSuggestionView(mixins.CreateModelMixin,

generics.GenericAPIView):
    queryset = Course.objects.none()   # prevent
list access
    serializer_class = CourseSerializer
    permission_classes = [IsAuthenticated]

    def post(self, request, *args, **kwargs):
        return self.create(request, *args,
**kwargs)

    def get(self, request, *args, **kwargs):
        return Response({'detail': 'Method not
allowed'}, status=405)
```

In this case:

You're allowing only POST `/api/course-suggestions/`

You've excluded listing and retrieving by not including those mixins

You're protecting the view with a permission class

You're explicitly handling unsupported methods

This kind of precise control is much harder with viewsets, which are opinionated and expect to support a full set of operations.

Building Your Own Custom Mixin

Mixins are reusable—not just from DRF, but also the ones you create.

Say you want to log the user and timestamp every time a course is retrieved, for audit purposes. Instead of repeating that logic in multiple views, you can build a custom mixin.

```
import logging
from rest_framework.response import Response

logger = logging.getLogger(__name__)

class AuditRetrieveMixin:
    def retrieve(self, request, *args, **kwargs):
        response = super().retrieve(request, *args,
**kwargs)
        user = request.user if
request.user.is_authenticated else 'Anonymous'
        logger.info(f"Course {kwargs.get('pk')}
retrieved by {user}")
        return response
```

Then use it with your view:

```
class AuditedCourseDetailView(AuditRetrieveMixin,

mixins.RetrieveModelMixin,

generics.GenericAPIView):
    queryset = Course.objects.all()
    serializer_class = CourseSerializer

    def get(self, request, *args, **kwargs):
```

```
        return self.retrieve(request, *args,
**kwargs)
```

This approach allows you to keep business logic encapsulated and easily testable. You can apply the same audit behavior to different models and views just by reusing your mixin.

Combining with GenericAPIView

`GenericAPIView` is the base class that powers all of DRF's generic views and viewsets. It gives you important tools like:

`get_queryset()` — override to customize object selection

`get_serializer_class()` — choose different serializers based on conditions

`get_serializer_context()` — pass additional context to your serializers

Here's how you can use it to show different serializers for authenticated users:

```
class CourseAccessView(mixins.RetrieveModelMixin,
                       generics.GenericAPIView):
    queryset = Course.objects.all()

    def get_serializer_class(self):
        if self.request.user.is_staff:
            return AdminCourseSerializer
        return PublicCourseSerializer

    def get(self, request, *args, **kwargs):
        return self.retrieve(request, *args,
**kwargs)
```

This approach gives you flexibility and structure. You keep your logic inside reusable components and apply them as needed.

Why Mixins Matter

Mixins allow you to:

Reuse behavior across multiple views without repeating yourself

Build lightweight, single-purpose views

96

Override or extend default behaviors in a controlled way

Compose views that only support the actions you want to expose

Avoid the rigidity of a full `ModelViewSet` when you only need partial functionality

They're also extremely useful when building internal or admin APIs, where you might expose certain operations that are too specific or sensitive for public endpoints.

So when you're deciding how to structure your views, remember: mixins give you the flexibility to **opt in to exactly what you need**—no more, no less.

Customizing View Behavior and Responses

The behavior of your views doesn't end with the choice of serializers or the mixins you apply. In real-world applications, you'll often need to tailor how your views behave—either to control what gets returned, how it's structured, or how it reacts to different conditions.

You might want to add metadata to a response, dynamically alter a queryset, return a non-standard HTTP status, or enforce additional rules based on the user or request context. Django REST Framework gives you a robust set of tools to do all of this cleanly and consistently.

At the core of every view is the queryset it uses to fetch data. While setting `queryset = Course.objects.all()` works for simple use cases, you'll often want to customize which records a user can access—especially when applying filters based on authentication or role.

Suppose you want users to see only their own courses, but admin users should see everything. Instead of duplicating logic in multiple views, override `get_queryset()`:

```
from .models import Course

class CourseViewSet(viewsets.ModelViewSet):
    serializer_class = CourseSerializer
```

```
    def get_queryset(self):
        user = self.request.user
        if user.is_staff:
            return Course.objects.all()
        return
Course.objects.filter(instructor=user)
```

This ensures that the same view behaves differently depending on who's accessing it. Your business logic stays centralized and easy to modify.

Passing Context into Serializers

Sometimes your serializer needs to know about the current user, or some detail of the request. DRF handles this using `get_serializer_context()`.

Let's say you want to display different content to staff users versus regular users. You can pass that context into the serializer:

```
class CourseViewSet(viewsets.ModelViewSet):
    queryset = Course.objects.all()
    serializer_class = CourseSerializer

    def get_serializer_context(self):
        context = super().get_serializer_context()
        context['is_admin'] =
self.request.user.is_staff
        return context
```

In your serializer:

```
class
CourseSerializer(serializers.ModelSerializer):
    class Meta:
        model = Course
        fields = ['id', 'title', 'description']

    def to_representation(self, instance):
        data = super().to_representation(instance)
        if self.context.get('is_admin'):
            data['internal_notes'] = 'This course
has unpublished content.'
        return data
```

98

Now the response adapts to who's making the request—without creating separate serializers or views.

Changing How Responses Are Returned

There are cases where the standard behavior of DRF isn't enough. For example, maybe you want to return a custom status code on update, or you want to return additional metadata along with the actual object.

Let's say you want to return a 202 Accepted status instead of 200 OK when updating a course—because some post-update processing happens asynchronously.

You override the `update()` method:

```
from rest_framework.response import Response
from rest_framework import status

class CourseViewSet(viewsets.ModelViewSet):
    queryset = Course.objects.all()
    serializer_class = CourseSerializer

    def update(self, request, *args, **kwargs):
        response = super().update(request, *args,
**kwargs)
        return Response({
            "message": "Course update accepted.
Processing in background.",
            "data": response.data
        }, status=status.HTTP_202_ACCEPTED)
```

This is useful for long-running updates or situations where the state of the object might not be final right after the request completes.

Injecting Additional Data into List Responses

There are times when you want to return extra data along with your list of results—like totals, filters, or metadata. DRF lets you control this by overriding the `list()` method.

Suppose you want to include a count of how many courses are returned:

```
class CourseViewSet(viewsets.ReadOnlyModelViewSet):
```

```
    queryset = Course.objects.all()
    serializer_class = CourseSerializer

    def list(self, request, *args, **kwargs):
        response = super().list(request, *args,
**kwargs)
        return Response({
            'count': len(response.data),
            'results': response.data
        })
```

This pattern is useful when building client-side dashboards or data tables that rely on supplementary information.

Conditionally Using Different Serializers

You don't always want to use the same serializer for all actions. For example, the data you return in a `list()` may be different from what you return in `retrieve()`.

Instead of splitting your views, use `get_serializer_class()` to return different serializers for different actions:

```
class CourseViewSet(viewsets.ModelViewSet):
    queryset = Course.objects.all()

    def get_serializer_class(self):
        if self.action == 'list':
            return PublicCourseSerializer
        return DetailedCourseSerializer
```

This approach keeps your code compact and respects the different needs of each endpoint. Your list view stays lightweight, while detail views can provide additional data like nested relationships or computed values.

Overriding Create and Destroy Behavior

When creating or deleting objects, you often want to perform some side effect: logging, sending an email, or assigning a default value.

You can do this cleanly with `perform_create()` and `perform_destroy()`:

```
class CourseViewSet(viewsets.ModelViewSet):
```

```
    . . .

    def perform_create(self, serializer):
        # Automatically assign the logged-in user
as instructor

serializer.save(instructor=self.request.user)

    def perform_destroy(self, instance):
        # Log deletion or clean up related objects
        instance.delete()
        logger.info(f"Course {instance.title} was
deleted by {self.request.user}")
```

You're not overriding the whole `create()` or `destroy()` logic—just injecting what matters to your business logic.

Customizing Error Responses

Sometimes you want to customize how errors are returned from your API— either to provide more user-friendly messages or to wrap them in a structure that fits your frontend framework.

Instead of modifying every view, define a global exception handler.

Create a file `api/exception_handler.py`:

```
from rest_framework.views import import exception_handler

def custom_exception_handler(exc, context):
    response = exception_handler(exc, context)

    if response is not None:
        response.data = {
            'status': 'error',
            'errors': response.data
        }

    return response
```

Then set it in your settings:

```
# settings.py
```

```
REST_FRAMEWORK = {
    'EXCEPTION_HANDLER':
'api.exception_handler.custom_exception_handler',
}
```

Now all your validation and server errors return a predictable structure:

```
{
  "status": "error",
  "errors": {
    "title": ["This field is required."]
  }
}
```

This keeps your frontend team happy and your API consistent.

View customization in DRF is not just about aesthetics. It's about aligning your API with your business logic. You get to:

Control what data is shown and who sees it

Modify how serializers behave under different conditions

Adjust the structure and semantics of responses

Inject custom behavior into standard operations

Build APIs that adapt intelligently to users, requests, and actions

These capabilities give you full control without forcing you to sacrifice the structure and power of DRF's built-in abstractions.

In the next chapter, we'll explore authentication and permissions—because once your API has structure, logic, and behavior, the next step is ensuring that access to those resources is secure, intentional, and auditable. But with the tools you've just learned, you're now ready to build views that don't just return data—they return the right data, in the right way, under the right conditions.

Chapter 5: Authentication, Permissions, and Security

Everything you've built so far—your models, serializers, and views—forms the backbone of your API. But without security, none of it can be trusted. That's not just about keeping intruders out. It's about making sure the right users have access to the right resources, at the right time, for the right reasons.

In this chapter, we're going to walk through how Django REST Framework handles **authentication**, **permissions**, and **security**. You'll learn how to integrate Django's built-in user system, implement token and JWT-based authentication, write custom permission classes, structure role-based access, and secure endpoints with rate limiting and throttling.

Security is not something to be bolted on after the fact. It's an essential part of designing a professional-grade API.

Django's Built-In User Model and Auth System

Before you think about tokens, JWTs, or any advanced security flow in Django REST Framework, it's important that you're completely familiar with Django's built-in authentication system. This is the backbone of identity in Django, and it's also the part DRF depends on to manage authentication and permissions.

Django ships with a complete user model that includes all the essentials—username, email, password hashing, permissions, groups, and superuser support. Even if you plan to extend it or replace it later, understanding how it works is non-negotiable. It's the first building block in every secure Django API.

Out of the box, Django provides a `User` model that lives in `django.contrib.auth.models`. You can import it directly, but it's better practice to use Django's utility function:

```
from django.contrib.auth import get_user_model
```

```
User = get_user_model()
```

This approach ensures compatibility in case you're using a custom user model, which we'll cover shortly.

By default, the `User` model includes the following fields:

`username`: a unique string used for login

`email`: an optional email field

`password`: a hashed password, never stored in plaintext

`is_staff`: designates admin panel access

`is_active`: flags whether the account is enabled

`is_superuser`: grants all permissions

`date_joined`: timestamp of account creation

It also includes a permission system and group support, which lets you assign roles or manage fine-grained access rules later.

If you're using Django's default user model, creating a user in the shell looks like this:

```
python manage.py shell
from django.contrib.auth.models import User

user = User.objects.create_user(username='john',
password='securepass123')
```

You can also use `create_superuser()` to make an admin user:

```
User.objects.create_superuser(username='admin',
password='adminpass', email='admin@example.com')
```

This user will have full access to the Django admin site and any restricted API views using `IsAdminUser` in DRF.

Passwords are stored using Django's password hashers, not in plaintext. When you set a password using `create_user()` or `set_password()`, it's automatically hashed using the currently configured algorithm—by default, PBKDF2 with SHA256.

Authenticating Users

Django includes a simple `authenticate()` function that you can use to verify credentials:

```
from django.contrib.auth import authenticate

user = authenticate(username='john',
password='securepass123')
if user:
    print("Authenticated")
else:
    print("Invalid credentials")
```

If the credentials are correct, `authenticate()` returns a user object. If not, it returns `None`. You'll often see this used in login views, or when implementing token or JWT-based authentication.

Django also provides a `login()` and `logout()` mechanism for session-based authentication, which is useful for browser-based apps but less relevant in pure REST APIs where token-based auth is more common.

Customizing the User Model

One of the best practices in Django is to define your own user model from the beginning, even if the default one is "good enough" for now. This future-proofs your project in case you want to use email instead of username, or store profile fields like `phone_number`, `role`, or `organization`.

To do this, subclass `AbstractUser` or `AbstractBaseUser`. Here's the simplest example using `AbstractUser`:

```
# accounts/models.py

from django.contrib.auth.models import AbstractUser
from django.db import models

class CustomUser(AbstractUser):
```

```
    phone_number = models.CharField(max_length=15,
blank=True)
```

Then, in your settings:

```
# settings.py

AUTH_USER_MODEL = 'accounts.CustomUser'
```

Make sure you configure this before running `migrate` for the first time, otherwise it's difficult to change later without resetting your database.

This model includes all the behavior of the original user model, but with your custom fields added. You can now use this in DRF views and serializers just like the default one.

Using the User Model in Serializers

Let's say you want to expose a list of users to admin staff. Here's a serializer that shows basic user data:

```
# accounts/serializers.py

from django.contrib.auth import get_user_model
from rest_framework import serializers

User = get_user_model()

class UserSerializer(serializers.ModelSerializer):
    class Meta:
        model = User
        fields = ['id', 'username', 'email',
'is_active']
```

This will convert user model instances into JSON like:

```
{
  "id": 1,
  "username": "john",
  "email": "john@example.com",
  "is_active": true
}
```

You can use this serializer in a view that's restricted to admin users:

```python
# accounts/views.py

from rest_framework import viewsets
from rest_framework.permissions import IsAdminUser
from .serializers import UserSerializer
from django.contrib.auth import get_user_model

User = get_user_model()

class UserViewSet(viewsets.ReadOnlyModelViewSet):
    queryset = User.objects.all()
    serializer_class = UserSerializer
    permission_classes = [IsAdminUser]
```

Wire this into your router, and you now have a secure, read-only API endpoint for listing users—only accessible by admins.

Working with the Auth System in APIs

When a user makes a request to your API, DRF provides the authenticated user object at `request.user`. This allows you to implement business logic and access rules based on the user identity.

Here's a practical example from a course creation view:

```python
class CourseViewSet(viewsets.ModelViewSet):
    serializer_class = CourseSerializer

    def get_queryset(self):
        return
Course.objects.filter(instructor=self.request.user)

    def perform_create(self, serializer):

serializer.save(instructor=self.request.user)
```

This ensures that:

A user only sees their own courses

When creating a course, the instructor is automatically set to the logged-in user

You don't need to send the instructor ID in the request body. That logic is enforced at the view level, which simplifies the frontend and prevents privilege escalation.

Django's built-in user model and authentication system give you a strong foundation for user management. Whether you're sticking with the default model or defining your own, the structure supports secure password handling, role flags (`is_staff`, `is_superuser`), user lookups, and permission enforcement.

This system integrates cleanly with Django REST Framework, and everything else you build—token authentication, JWT, permissions, and role-based access—will rely on this structure.

Token Authentication and JWT Integration

Django REST Framework is designed to support different authentication mechanisms out of the box, and one of the most commonly used in APIs is **token-based authentication**. It's simple, stateless, and integrates smoothly with most client-side applications, mobile apps, and external services.

In this section, you'll learn how to implement two different but related token-based systems in Django REST Framework:

DRF's default Token Authentication

JWT (JSON Web Tokens) with `djangorestframework-simplejwt`

You'll get hands-on examples, step-by-step setup, and practical advice on choosing and using both methods effectively.

Token Authentication with DRF's Built-In System

Token authentication is provided by the `rest_framework.authtoken` module. Each user is assigned a unique token that's used to authenticate their requests. That token can be passed in the `Authorization` header for every API call.

Installation and Setup

Make sure `rest_framework.authtoken` is added to your installed apps:

```
# settings.py

INSTALLED_APPS = [
    ...
    'rest_framework',
    'rest_framework.authtoken',
]
```

Run the migrations to create the table for storing tokens:

```
python manage.py migrate
```

You can now generate tokens for users. You can do this manually from the shell:

```
python manage.py shell
from django.contrib.auth import get_user_model
from rest_framework.authtoken.models import Token

User = get_user_model()
user = User.objects.get(username='jane')
token, created =
Token.objects.get_or_create(user=user)
print(token.key)
```

This token should be stored securely by the client, and included in each request header like this:

```
Authorization: Token
3f4f8e9a7d99a8f9fcbf76c1a8c34cd45662bdff
```

Exposing a Token Login Endpoint

You can make token retrieval dynamic by enabling a login endpoint.

Add this to your `urls.py`:

```
from rest_framework.authtoken.views import
obtain_auth_token

urlpatterns = [
```

```
    path('api/token/', obtain_auth_token),
]
```

Now clients can POST their credentials to `/api/token/`:

```
{
  "username": "jane",
  "password": "password123"
}
```

And receive a response like:

```
{
  "token":
"3f4f8e9a7d99a8f9fcbf76c1a8c34cd45662bdff"
}
```

This works well for simple use cases, internal APIs, and systems where tokens can be revoked or replaced easily. However, for distributed systems or mobile apps that require stateless authentication, you'll likely want something more scalable and secure—like **JWT**.

JWT Authentication with SimpleJWT

JSON Web Tokens (JWT) are compact, URL-safe tokens that contain encoded data. They're signed using a secret key or a public/private key pair, which allows both the client and server to verify their integrity without requiring a server-side session or token table.

Django REST Framework doesn't include JWT support by default, but it integrates well with the widely used SimpleJWT package.

Installing SimpleJWT

Start by installing the package:

```
pip install djangorestframework-simplejwt
```

Then update your settings:

```
# settings.py

REST_FRAMEWORK = {
    'DEFAULT_AUTHENTICATION_CLASSES': [
```

```
'rest_framework_simplejwt.authentication.JWTAuthent
ication',
    ]
}
```

Adding Token Endpoints

Now add the login and refresh endpoints to your `urls.py`:

```
from rest_framework_simplejwt.views import (
    TokenObtainPairView,
    TokenRefreshView,
)

urlpatterns = [
    path('api/token/',
TokenObtainPairView.as_view(),
name='token_obtain_pair'),
    path('api/token/refresh/',
TokenRefreshView.as_view(), name='token_refresh'),
]
```

Clients can now send a POST request to `/api/token/` with their credentials:

```
{
  "username": "jane",
  "password": "password123"
}
```

The response contains two tokens:

```
{
  "refresh": "eyJ0eXAiOiJKV1QiLCJhbGci...",
  "access": "eyJ0eXAiOiJKV1QiLCJhbGci..."
}
```

The **access token** is short-lived (default 5 minutes) and used to authenticate requests.

The **refresh token** is long-lived (default 1 day) and is used to get a new access token without logging in again.

To authenticate, the client includes the access token in the header:

```
Authorization: Bearer eyJ0eXAiOiJKV1QiLCJhbGci...
```

When the access token expires, the client sends the refresh token to
`/api/token/refresh/`:

```
{
   "refresh": "eyJ0eXAiOiJKV1QiLCJhbGci..."
}
```

And receives a new access token in return.

Protecting Views with Authentication

Whether you're using token auth or JWT, protecting your views is the same.
Just apply `IsAuthenticated`:

```python
from rest_framework.permissions import
IsAuthenticated

class CourseViewSet(viewsets.ModelViewSet):
    queryset = Course.objects.all()
    serializer_class = CourseSerializer
    permission_classes = [IsAuthenticated]

    def get_queryset(self):
        return
Course.objects.filter(instructor=self.request.user)
```

Only authenticated users can now access these endpoints, and you can filter
data based on the current user using `request.user`.

You can also allow public read access while requiring authentication for
writes:

```python
from rest_framework.permissions import
IsAuthenticatedOrReadOnly
```

This is useful for public APIs like blog posts, articles, or course listings, where
anyone can read but only logged-in users can create or update.

Configuring Token Expiry and Rotation

SimpleJWT gives you full control over expiration and token rotation. You can
customize this in your settings:

```
from datetime import timedelta

SIMPLE_JWT = {
    'ACCESS_TOKEN_LIFETIME': timedelta(minutes=15),
    'REFRESH_TOKEN_LIFETIME': timedelta(days=1),
    'ROTATE_REFRESH_TOKENS': True,
    'BLACKLIST_AFTER_ROTATION': True,
}
```

When `ROTATE_REFRESH_TOKENS` is enabled, each refresh request returns a new refresh token. If you enable blacklisting, old refresh tokens become invalid.

This prevents replay attacks and makes your authentication system more secure in long-lived sessions.

Choosing Between Token and JWT

Use Token Authentication if:

You're building internal or trusted system-to-system APIs

You prefer to store and manage tokens in the database

You need server-side revocation or easy manual token resets

Use JWT if:

You need stateless authentication across distributed services

You're building mobile or single-page apps

You want access and refresh token flows for better session control

Both options work well with Django REST Framework. What matters most is your architecture, your clients, and your operational needs.

Token-based authentication is a critical step toward building a secure, scalable API. Whether you choose DRF's built-in token system or the more advanced JWT strategy, you now have the tools to manage authentication safely and effectively.

In the next section, we'll build on this by defining **custom permissions**—rules that decide who can access what—so that your API doesn't just know who a user is, but also what they're allowed to do.

Writing Custom Permissions and Access Rules

Authentication identifies who the user is. Permissions decide what that user is allowed to do. While authentication checks credentials, permissions define access—who can read, write, update, or delete data, and under what conditions.

Django REST Framework gives you a powerful and flexible permissions system. It includes a set of built-in permission classes, but more importantly, it gives you the ability to define your own, so you can express rules that are unique to your application.

The Role of Permissions in a View

Permissions are evaluated at two levels:

Global permissions, which are checked before the view's logic runs.

Object-level permissions, which are checked when accessing a specific object instance—usually during retrieve, update, or delete operations.

Every permission class must inherit from `rest_framework.permissions.BasePermission`, and implement either `has_permission()` for global checks or `has_object_permission()` for object-level checks.

A Real-World Example: Course Ownership

Let's say you're building a platform where instructors can create courses. Only the creator (the instructor) should be allowed to update or delete their own course. Other users can view courses, but not modify them.

Here's how you could express that in a permission class:

```
# permissions.py

from rest_framework.permissions import
BasePermission, SAFE_METHODS
```

```
class IsOwnerOrReadOnly(BasePermission):
    """
    Allows full access to the owner of the object.
    Read-only access for everyone else.
    """

    def has_object_permission(self, request, view,
obj):
        if request.method in SAFE_METHODS:
            return True
        return obj.instructor == request.user
```

This allows any user (authenticated or not) to read course data (GET, HEAD, OPTIONS), but only the instructor who created the course can modify or delete it (PUT, PATCH, DELETE).

In your CourseViewSet, you apply this permission:

```
from rest_framework.viewsets import ModelViewSet
from .models import Course
from .serializers import CourseSerializer
from .permissions import IsOwnerOrReadOnly

class CourseViewSet(ModelViewSet):
    queryset = Course.objects.all()
    serializer_class = CourseSerializer
    permission_classes = [IsOwnerOrReadOnly]
```

This is all you need to enforce proper ownership logic at the API level— secure, reusable, and easy to test.

Global Access Rules with has_permission

Now let's say you want to restrict creation of courses so that only users with the role 'instructor' can create them. But anyone should be able to list or retrieve them.

That kind of rule is handled with has_permission():

```
class IsInstructorCreateOnly(BasePermission):
    """
    Only instructors can create courses.
    Other methods are unrestricted.
```

```
"""

    def has_permission(self, request, view):
        if request.method == 'POST':
            return request.user.is_authenticated
and request.user.role == 'instructor'
        return True
```

This class is evaluated before the view tries to create anything. You can combine it with other permissions if needed:

```
class CourseViewSet(ModelViewSet):
    permission_classes = [IsInstructorCreateOnly,
IsOwnerOrReadOnly]
```

This gives you global control over creation, plus object-level control over update and delete operations.

Combining Multiple Permissions

You can combine multiple permission classes by passing them in a list. DRF evaluates them with an **AND** condition—all permission classes must grant access for the request to proceed.

If you want **OR** behavior, you need to write a wrapper yourself.

For example:

```
class IsAdminOrInstructor(BasePermission):
    def has_permission(self, request, view):
        return (
            request.user.is_authenticated and
            (request.user.is_staff or
request.user.role == 'instructor')
        )
```

This pattern allows you to build roles like "admin OR instructor" in one place, and reuse that permission class across multiple views.

Permissions with Querysets and View Context

Sometimes, your permission depends not just on the object, but on something from the request or view. DRF makes the request and view available inside your permission methods.

Let's say you want to allow users to delete a course only if it has no enrollments:

```python
class CanDeleteEmptyCourse(BasePermission):
    def has_object_permission(self, request, view, obj):
        if request.method != 'DELETE':
            return True
        return obj.enrollments.count() == 0
```

This lets the delete action go through only if the course has zero enrollments. You can apply this to `CourseViewSet` the same way as before.

Writing a Permission that Applies to Related Models

Let's say you're building an enrollment system. You want to ensure a student can only enroll themselves—not other users.

Here's a permission that checks that condition:

```python
class IsStudentSelf(BasePermission):
    def has_permission(self, request, view):
        if request.method == 'POST':
            student_id = request.data.get('student')
            return str(request.user.id) == str(student_id)
        return True
```

This assumes the client is sending a `student` field in the payload, which must match the ID of the authenticated user. You can enforce this in a serializer as well, but placing it in a permission keeps your logic centralized and ensures no bypass via manually crafted requests.

Testing Your Custom Permissions

Testing permissions is straightforward and essential.

Here's an example using Django's test client:

```
from rest_framework.test import APIClient
from django.contrib.auth import get_user_model
from .models import Course

User = get_user_model()

def test_only_owner_can_delete_course():
    user1 =
User.objects.create_user(username='owner',
password='test')
    user2 =
User.objects.create_user(username='other',
password='test')

    course = Course.objects.create(title='Test',
instructor=user1)

    client = APIClient()
    client.force_authenticate(user=user2)
    response =
client.delete(f'/api/courses/{course.id}/')
    assert response.status_code == 403  # Forbidden
```

This ensures your permission is working as expected before deploying it into production.

Permissions are the contract between your API and the real world. They translate business rules into enforceable access policies. Django REST Framework gives you both structure and flexibility—whether you're implementing ownership checks, role enforcement, or conditional logic based on data or context.

To recap, you can:

Use `has_permission()` to enforce global rules

Use `has_object_permission()` to enforce instance-level rules

Combine multiple permissions logically

Test permissions in isolation using DRF's test tools

This pattern is powerful, reusable, and easy to evolve as your application grows. Now that your API can securely identify who the user is and what they're allowed to do, you're ready to scale your access rules further—across roles, groups, and more complex structures like **role-based access control**, which we'll explore next.

Role-Based Access Control (RBAC)

When your application grows beyond just admins and regular users, you'll need more than just basic permissions. You'll want a way to organize access based on roles—distinct sets of responsibilities, like `admin`, `instructor`, `student`, or `moderator`. That's where Role-Based Access Control (RBAC) becomes essential.

RBAC is about mapping what a user can do to what role they hold. It allows you to say, "Instructors can create and manage courses," or "Students can enroll in courses, but not delete them," and then enforce that logic cleanly throughout your API.

Django doesn't come with RBAC built in, but it gives you all the tools you need to implement it effectively. Django REST Framework plugs into this setup seamlessly, allowing you to build views and permission classes that respond to roles consistently and securely.

Defining Roles in Your User Model

Start by making sure your user model can store roles in a way that's easy to reason about and query.

If you're using a custom user model, you can define roles using a `CharField` with choices:

```
# accounts/models.py

from django.contrib.auth.models import AbstractUser
from django.db import models

class User(AbstractUser):
    ROLE_CHOICES = (
```

```
            ('admin', 'Admin'),
            ('instructor', 'Instructor'),
            ('student', 'Student'),
        )
        role = models.CharField(max_length=20,
choices=ROLE_CHOICES, default='student')
```

If you're extending the default `User` model via a profile or proxy model, you can apply similar logic through a related model.

Once added, this field is available on every user, and can be used to check role-based permissions in views, serializers, or custom logic.

Creating Role-Based Permissions

Now you need to enforce your roles in code. This is where DRF's permission system really helps. Let's write permission classes that check whether a user has the correct role for the task they're attempting.

Here's one for instructors:

```
# permissions.py

from rest_framework.permissions import
BasePermission

class IsInstructor(BasePermission):
    def has_permission(self, request, view):
        return request.user.is_authenticated and
request.user.role == 'instructor'
```

And here's one for admin-only access:

```
class IsAdmin(BasePermission):
    def has_permission(self, request, view):
        return request.user.is_authenticated and
request.user.role == 'admin'
```

Apply this in a view like this:

```
# courses/views.py

from rest_framework.viewsets import ModelViewSet
from .models import Course
```

```
from .serializers import CourseSerializer
from .permissions import IsInstructor

class CourseViewSet(ModelViewSet):
    queryset = Course.objects.all()
    serializer_class = CourseSerializer
    permission_classes = [IsInstructor]
```

Only users with role='instructor' will be allowed to create, update, or delete courses. This ensures your API logic respects the intended boundaries of responsibility.

Combining Roles and Object-Level Logic

You can layer RBAC with object-level permissions for more precise control. For example, instructors should only edit their own courses, but admins can edit any course.

Here's how you can build that into a permission class:

```
class IsInstructorOrAdminOwner(BasePermission):
    def has_object_permission(self, request, view,
obj):
        if request.user.role == 'admin':
            return True
        return obj.instructor == request.user and
request.user.role == 'instructor'
```

Apply it the same way:

```
class CourseViewSet(ModelViewSet):
    . . .
    permission_classes = [IsInstructorOrAdminOwner]
```

Now, instructors can only touch their own content, but admins can touch any. This respects both role and ownership.

Assigning Roles at Signup or via Admin

Roles are typically assigned when a user registers or when an admin manages users.

You can expose this via the Django admin by including the `role` field in your `UserAdmin`:

```python
# accounts/admin.py

from django.contrib import admin
from django.contrib.auth.admin import UserAdmin
from .models import User

class CustomUserAdmin(UserAdmin):
    fieldsets = UserAdmin.fieldsets + (
        ('Role', {'fields': ('role',)}),
    )

admin.site.register(User, CustomUserAdmin)
```

If you're handling user registration via an API, make sure the role assignment is controlled and validated. You likely don't want users registering as `admin` or `instructor` without authorization.

In your serializer:

```python
class
UserSignupSerializer(serializers.ModelSerializer):
    class Meta:
        model = User
        fields = ['username', 'password', 'email']
        extra_kwargs = {
            'password': {'write_only': True}
        }

    def create(self, validated_data):
        user =
User.objects.create_user(**validated_data)
        user.role = 'student'   # default role
        user.save()
        return user
```

This way, every new user starts as a `student`, unless an admin promotes them later.

Protecting Admin-Only Actions

Suppose you're building a moderation system, and you want only `admin` users to delete flagged content.

You could create a custom action in your viewset and protect it using `permission_classes`:

```
from rest_framework.decorators import action
from rest_framework.response import Response
from rest_framework import status

class CourseViewSet(ModelViewSet):
    . . .

    @action(detail=True, methods=['post'],
permission_classes=[IsAdmin])
    def archive(self, request, pk=None):
        course = self.get_object()
        course.is_archived = True
        course.save()
        return Response({'status': 'archived'},
status=status.HTTP_200_OK)
```

Only users with the admin role will be able to hit this route. All others will receive a `403 Forbidden`.

Reusing Roles Across Your Application

Once you start using RBAC, you'll find it helpful to group role-based logic into utilities you can reuse throughout your application.

Here's a helper function you can call in views or serializers:

```
def is_admin(user):
    return user.is_authenticated and user.role ==
'admin'

def is_instructor(user):
    return user.is_authenticated and user.role ==
'instructor'
```

Use these anywhere you need them—for filtering querysets, conditional validation, or context-aware serializer behavior:

```
class
CourseSerializer(serializers.ModelSerializer):
    class Meta:
        model = Course
        fields = '__all__'

    def validate(self, data):
        user = self.context['request'].user
        if is_student(user):
            raise
serializers.ValidationError("Students cannot create
courses.")
        return data
```

RBAC is how you translate your organization's policies into actual system behavior. It provides a scalable way to separate concerns and assign responsibility based on user roles.

In Django, you can implement RBAC by:

Adding a `role` field to your user model

Writing role-specific permission classes

Combining those permissions with object-level checks

Protecting views and actions with role-based logic

Testing access logic using DRF's permission hooks

This structure keeps your API secure, predictable, and easy to manage as your platform evolves. And because you're building your roles into the foundation of your project, you avoid hardcoding logic in individual views and keep your codebase clean and maintainable.

Rate Limiting, Throttling, and Securing Sensitive Endpoints

A secure API isn't just about who can access your data—it's also about how often, how quickly, and under what conditions they're allowed to do so. Rate limiting and throttling are two critical techniques used to control traffic to your

API and prevent abuse, whether that's from accidental overuse, bot traffic, or intentional denial-of-service attempts.

In Django REST Framework, throttling is built in. It allows you to define limits on how many requests a user or anonymous client can make in a given time window. You can apply throttles globally, per view, or per scope. This helps you protect login endpoints, user registration flows, data-heavy actions, and any part of your API that's vulnerable to spamming or brute-force attacks.

Why Throttling Matters

When your API is exposed to the public—whether for authenticated users or anonymous access—you must account for the cost of every request. Without rate limiting, even well-intentioned users can accidentally overwhelm your system.

Some examples of where throttling is critical:

A login endpoint that gets hit repeatedly with failed credentials

A search endpoint that performs expensive database queries

A background task trigger or webhook processor that could be abused

Any public-facing endpoint accessible without authentication

Rate limiting controls the volume. Throttling enforces the rules.

Enabling Throttling in Django REST Framework

To get started, add throttling classes to your DRF settings:

```python
# settings.py

REST_FRAMEWORK = {
    'DEFAULT_THROTTLE_CLASSES': [

'rest_framework.throttling.UserRateThrottle',

'rest_framework.throttling.AnonRateThrottle',
    ],
    'DEFAULT_THROTTLE_RATES': {
        'user': '1000/day',
        'anon': '25/hour',
```

```
        }
    }
```

Here's what this means:

UserRateThrottle applies to authenticated users, keyed by their user ID.

AnonRateThrottle applies to unauthenticated users, typically keyed by IP address.

Rates can be expressed in `second`, `minute`, `hour`, or `day`.

These limits are enforced globally by default, meaning every view in your API will honor them unless you override them explicitly.

You can test this quickly using Django's built-in test client or a tool like Postman. Once the limit is hit, the client will receive a `429 Too Many Requests` response.

```
{
  "detail": "Request was throttled. Expected
available in 56 seconds."
}
```

This message is returned automatically by DRF's throttle classes.

Using Scoped Throttling for Fine-Grained Control

Global throttling is helpful, but you'll often need more control—especially for protecting individual endpoints.

Scoped throttling lets you define a throttle scope per view. First, enable the class:

```
# settings.py

REST_FRAMEWORK = {
    'DEFAULT_THROTTLE_CLASSES': [

'rest_framework.throttling.ScopedRateThrottle',
    ],
    'DEFAULT_THROTTLE_RATES': {
        'login': '5/minute',
        'search': '60/hour',
```

```
        }
}
```

Now apply the scope in your view:

```
from rest_framework.throttling import
ScopedRateThrottle
from rest_framework.views import APIView
from rest_framework.response import Response

class LoginView(APIView):
    throttle_classes = [ScopedRateThrottle]
    throttle_scope = 'login'

    def post(self, request):
        # authentication logic
        return Response({"message": "Login
successful"})
```

This limits clients to five login attempts per minute, regardless of their global throttle. You can define different scopes for other views, like password reset or newsletter signup.

Creating Custom Throttling Logic

If you need custom behavior—for example, a different limit for premium users or a dynamic rule based on request data—you can write your own throttle class.

Here's how to give staff users unlimited requests and throttle everyone else:

```
from rest_framework.throttling import
UserRateThrottle

class StaffExemptThrottle(UserRateThrottle):
    def allow_request(self, request, view):
        if request.user.is_authenticated and
request.user.is_staff:
            return True  # unlimited for staff
        return super().allow_request(request, view)
```

Apply it to your views just like any other throttle class:

```
class ProtectedView(APIView):
    throttle_classes = [StaffExemptThrottle]
```

You can build on this pattern to support different subscription tiers, special APIs for mobile apps, or throttles based on country or IP range.

Securing Sensitive Endpoints

Certain endpoints in your API deserve extra attention beyond simple throttling:

Authentication endpoints (login, token, password reset)

User registration

Webhook consumers

Payment or transaction processing

For these routes, combine throttling with input validation, logging, and strict access checks.

Here's a password reset endpoint protected by throttling and strict method enforcement:

```
class PasswordResetView(APIView):
    throttle_classes = [ScopedRateThrottle]
    throttle_scope = 'password_reset'

    def post(self, request):
        email = request.data.get('email')
        if not email:
            return Response({"error": "Email is
required"}, status=400)

        # Validate that user exists, trigger reset
logic
        return Response({"message": "If your email
is registered, a reset link was sent."})
```

This view doesn't expose whether a user exists—preventing user enumeration—and throttles repeated requests from the same client.

Other ways to lock down sensitive endpoints:

Require re-authentication or password confirmation

Audit access via logs or analytics

Apply stricter rate limits than public endpoints

Add captchas (for browser-based flows)

If your API supports `DELETE` or `PATCH` operations, consider whether those should be throttled or require elevated privileges.

Checking Throttle Status in Code

If you want to inspect whether a user is being throttled—for example, to adjust UI behavior or debug an issue—you can access it from within the view:

```
if self.throttled(request):
    wait = self.get_throttles()[0].wait()
    return Response({'error': f'Please wait {wait}
seconds'}, status=429)
```

But DRF handles this automatically in most cases. You only need to use this if you're building custom behaviors or returning alternative messages.

Throttling is not just a performance measure—it's a security tool. By limiting how frequently requests can be made, you protect your API from brute-force attacks, denial-of-service attempts, and accidental misuse.

With DRF, you can:

Set global limits for all users or anonymous access

Define fine-grained scoped throttles per endpoint

Write custom logic to account for roles or behaviors

Secure endpoints with thoughtful request handling

Return clear error messages when limits are exceeded

Good throttling design keeps your API stable, predictable, and trustworthy. It's one of the last lines of defense against abuse, and when used correctly, it ensures that your API remains reliable for the users who count on it.

With authentication, permissions, role-based access, and throttling in place, your API is now professionally structured and well protected. In the next chapter, we'll explore filtering, searching, pagination, and parameterized endpoints—so your API isn't just secure, but also efficient and pleasant to consume.

Chapter 6: Querying, Filtering, and Pagination

Building a secure and functional API is the first half of the job. The second half is making that API usable and efficient—especially when your database grows, your data becomes relational, and your clients need to retrieve information in specific ways. That's where query control becomes essential.

In this chapter, we're going to work through the key aspects of querying and filtering in Django REST Framework: filtering records using URL parameters, enabling search and ordering, working with nested resources, applying pagination, and optimizing database queries for performance.

These are not optional features in a production API. They are what make your endpoints actually useful to frontend apps, third-party clients, mobile apps, or internal services that consume your API.

Filtering with Django Filter Backend

When you're building APIs that return collections of data—lists of users, articles, orders, courses, or anything else—one of the first requirements you'll hear from frontend developers is: "Can we filter this by category, status, or user?"

Hardcoding filters into each view quickly becomes messy and inconsistent. You need a systematic way to support flexible filtering, and Django REST Framework doesn't include this functionality natively—but it provides seamless integration with `django-filter`, a package designed exactly for this purpose.

The `DjangoFilterBackend` lets you filter your querysets based on the incoming query parameters, without writing repetitive code in each view. And it does this using a clean, declarative style that integrates tightly with your models.

Installing and Configuring `django-filter`

Start by installing the package:

```
pip install django-filter
```
Once installed, add it to your project's installed apps:

```
# settings.py

INSTALLED_APPS = [
    ...
    'django_filters',
]
```

Now tell Django REST Framework to use `DjangoFilterBackend` as one of its default filter backends:

```
# settings.py

REST_FRAMEWORK = {
    'DEFAULT_FILTER_BACKENDS': [

'django_filters.rest_framework.DjangoFilterBackend'
    ]
}
```

This global setting means any view or viewset that supports filtering will automatically use `DjangoFilterBackend`, unless you override it explicitly.

Filtering Basic Fields Using `filterset_fields`

The most straightforward way to enable filtering in a viewset is to define `filterset_fields`.

Let's say you're working with a `Course` model like this:

```
# courses/models.py

from django.db import models
from django.contrib.auth import get_user_model

User = get_user_model()

class Course(models.Model):
    title = models.CharField(max_length=255)
    is_published =
models.BooleanField(default=False)
```

```
    category = models.CharField(max_length=100)
    instructor = models.ForeignKey(User,
on_delete=models.CASCADE)
    publish_date = models.DateField()
```

Now you want to allow users of your API to filter the list of courses by is_published, category, and instructor.

In your viewset:

```
# courses/views.py

from rest_framework import viewsets
from .models import Course
from .serializers import CourseSerializer

class CourseViewSet(viewsets.ModelViewSet):
    queryset = Course.objects.all()
    serializer_class = CourseSerializer
    filterset_fields = ['is_published', 'category',
'instructor']
```

This enables simple filtering through URL parameters:

GET /api/courses/?is_published=true

GET /api/courses/?category=backend

GET /api/courses/?instructor=3

Django Filter automatically builds the filters based on the model fields and data types. For Boolean fields, you can pass true or false; for foreign keys, you pass the primary key value of the related model.

This setup requires almost no effort and immediately makes your API more useful.

Writing a Custom FilterSet Class

When you need more advanced filtering logic—like filtering by date ranges or using more expressive lookups—you can define a custom FilterSet.

Here's how you might let users filter courses between a start and end publish date:

```
# courses/filters.py

import django_filters
from .models import Course

class CourseFilter(django_filters.FilterSet):
    start_date =
django_filters.DateFilter(field_name='publish_date'
, lookup_expr='gte')
    end_date =
django_filters.DateFilter(field_name='publish_date'
, lookup_expr='lte')

    class Meta:
        model = Course
        fields = ['is_published', 'category',
'instructor']
```

Then update your viewset to use this filter class:

```
from .filters import CourseFilter

class CourseViewSet(viewsets.ModelViewSet):
    queryset = Course.objects.all()
    serializer_class = CourseSerializer
    filterset_class = CourseFilter
```

Your API now supports filtering courses like this:

```
GET /api/courses/?start_date=2024-01-
01&end_date=2024-12-31
```

This is especially useful in admin dashboards or analytics dashboards where users need time-based filtering.

Supporting Multiple Values

Django Filter allows you to accept multiple values for a single field using the `BaseInFilter` class. For example, if a user wants to filter by several categories:

```
class CharInFilter(django_filters.BaseInFilter,
django_filters.CharFilter):
```

```
    pass

class CourseFilter(django_filters.FilterSet):
    category = CharInFilter(field_name='category',
lookup_expr='in')

    class Meta:
        model = Course
        fields = ['category']
```

Now your clients can send:

```
GET /api/courses/?category=backend,frontend
```

And get back all courses whose category is either `backend` or `frontend`.

This kind of multi-value filtering is essential for building faceted search interfaces, where users can click multiple filters and see results update accordingly.

Case-Insensitive Filtering and Custom Lookups

Django Filter supports a wide range of lookup expressions, just like the Django ORM. You can apply case-insensitive lookups, partial matches, or negations.

For example, to enable filtering where the course title contains a certain keyword, regardless of case:

```
title_contains =
django_filters.CharFilter(field_name='title',
lookup_expr='icontains')
```

You can combine this with other filters or write completely custom logic by overriding the `filter_<fieldname>` method inside your `FilterSet`.

Filtering on Related Fields

You're not limited to filtering fields on the model itself—you can also filter on related fields.

Let's say you want to filter courses by the instructor's username:

```
class CourseFilter(django_filters.FilterSet):
```

135

```
    instructor_username =
django_filters.CharFilter(field_name='instructor__u
sername', lookup_expr='icontains')

    class Meta:
        model = Course
        fields = ['instructor_username']
```

This allows requests like:

```
GET /api/courses/?instructor_username=ade
```
This is incredibly powerful when your relationships span multiple models but your clients only know or care about user-facing fields like usernames, slugs, or human-readable labels.

Returning Filtered Results in the API

All of the filtering logic works seamlessly with your serializers and pagination. For example, using the above filters, your API will return paginated, filtered results like this:

```
{
  "count": 3,
  "next": null,
  "previous": null,
  "results": [
    {
      "id": 12,
      "title": "Fullstack Django",
      "category": "backend",
      "instructor": 3,
      "publish_date": "2024-06-01",
      "is_published": true
    },
    ...
  ]
}
```

Clients get a consistent structure, and you don't have to write extra view logic for filtering. It all happens automatically, based on the query parameters and your filter configuration.

Filtering is one of those API features that clients immediately notice if it's missing—and developers appreciate when it's implemented cleanly. With `django-filter` and DRF's `DjangoFilterBackend`, you can support everything from basic boolean filters to complex range queries and multi-value inputs, all without cluttering your views or serializers.

Key takeaways:

Use `filterset_fields` for quick, model-based filters

Use custom `FilterSet` classes for expressive and reusable filter logic

Support advanced filtering with `lookup_expr`, related fields, and `in` filters

Keep your API responses clean and predictable, even when filters are applied

Once your filtering is in place, your API becomes significantly more useful—not just for frontend developers but for power users, search interfaces, and integrations that need specific slices of your data. And because filtering runs at the queryset level, it remains efficient and scalable as your database grows.

Searching and Ordering API Results

Once you've exposed endpoints that return collections of data—like a list of courses, blog posts, or users—clients almost always want two things beyond basic filtering: the ability to **search** through records using keywords, and the ability to **control the order** in which those records appear.

Django REST Framework makes both tasks straightforward using two built-in filter backends: `SearchFilter` and `OrderingFilter`. These tools give your API consumers more control and allow you to support rich data discovery features without writing additional logic inside your views.

Enabling Search in DRF

Searching in DRF is not the same as full-text search with relevance scoring or ranked results. By default, DRF search performs simple case-insensitive containment checks (like Django's `icontains` query) on specified fields.

To start using it, you need to include `SearchFilter` in your project's settings:

```
# settings.py

REST_FRAMEWORK = {
    'DEFAULT_FILTER_BACKENDS': [

'django_filters.rest_framework.DjangoFilterBackend'
,
        'rest_framework.filters.SearchFilter',
    ]
}
```

You can also set it explicitly in each view if you want per-view control.

Now, let's say you have a `Course` model like this:

```
class Course(models.Model):
    title = models.CharField(max_length=255)
    description = models.TextField()
    category = models.CharField(max_length=100)
```

You want users to be able to search for courses by title and description.

In your viewset:

```
from rest_framework import filters

class CourseViewSet(viewsets.ModelViewSet):
    queryset = Course.objects.all()
    serializer_class = CourseSerializer
    filter_backends = [filters.SearchFilter]
    search_fields = ['title', 'description']
```

Now, the client can search like this:

```
GET /api/courses/?search=python
```

This will return all courses where `title` or `description` contains the word `python`, case-insensitive. Under the hood, DRF translates this to a SQL query using `icontains`, which is efficient enough for most use cases when used on indexed fields.

Search Syntax and Behavior

You can modify how each field behaves by using search prefixes.

For example, suppose you want to ensure that the title search only matches entries that start with a certain value. You'd prefix it with ^:

```
search_fields = ['^title', 'description']
```

Here's what the prefixes mean:

No prefix (default): case-insensitive containment (`icontains`)

^: starts-with lookup (`istartswith`)

=: exact match (`iexact`)

@: full-text search (only on PostgreSQL)

So with this configuration:

```
search_fields = ['^title', '=category']
```

These searches are now possible:

`GET /api/courses/?search=Intro`

This matches any title starting with "Intro".

`GET /api/courses/?search=backend`

This will only return courses where `category == 'backend'` exactly, case-insensitively.

Note that DRF applies search across all specified fields. So if you specify both `title` and `description`, a match in either field is considered valid.

Using Search with Related Fields

You're not limited to filtering on the model's direct fields. You can search across related fields using Django ORM-style double underscores.

Suppose each course is linked to an instructor (a `User` model), and you want to allow searching by the instructor's username:

```
search_fields = ['title', 'description',
'instructor__username']
```

Now users can search:

```
GET /api/courses/?search=janedoe
```

And this will return all courses where the instructor's username contains "janedoe".

This kind of flexibility is invaluable when building user-facing search tools or admin dashboards where the client wants to look up content created by specific users.

Combining Search with Filtering

DRF allows you to use `SearchFilter` alongside `DjangoFilterBackend`. You can combine both in the same view:

```
filter_backends = [

django_filters.rest_framework.DjangoFilterBackend,
    filters.SearchFilter
]

filterset_fields = ['category', 'is_published']
search_fields = ['title', 'description']
```

This allows clients to send structured filters and free-text search in the same request:

```
GET /api/courses/?category=backend&search=django
```

This returns all backend courses where either the title or description contains the word "django".

Enabling Ordering

Ordering allows clients to specify the sort order of results. It works just like Django's `.order_by()` in the ORM, and can be enabled using the `OrderingFilter`.

In your view:

```
filter_backends = [filters.OrderingFilter]
ordering_fields = ['publish_date', 'title']
ordering = ['publish_date']   # default ordering
```

Now clients can request results ordered by publish date or title:

```
GET /api/courses/?ordering=title
GET /api/courses/?ordering=-publish_date
```

The minus sign reverses the order—just like in a Django ORM query.

You can expose more fields to allow broader ordering, or restrict it to only the most relevant ones. Avoid exposing fields that aren't indexed or that are expensive to sort, as that can lead to performance issues with large datasets.

Combining Ordering with Search and Filtering

All these features work together when you configure multiple filter backends. You can layer filtering, search, and ordering in the same request.

```
filter_backends = [

django_filters.rest_framework.DjangoFilterBackend,
    filters.SearchFilter,
    filters.OrderingFilter,
]

filterset_fields = ['is_published', 'category']
search_fields = ['title', 'description']
ordering_fields = ['publish_date', 'title']
ordering = ['publish_date']
```

Now your API supports rich client interactions:

```
GET
/api/courses/?category=frontend&search=vue&ordering
=-title
```

This returns frontend courses where title or description contains "vue", sorted by title descending.

This pattern is easy to understand, doesn't require you to write custom logic in the view, and keeps your API logic declarative and maintainable.

With `SearchFilter` and `OrderingFilter`, Django REST Framework gives you a powerful yet simple way to let API clients explore your data the way they need to. These tools make your endpoints flexible without adding bloat or complexity to your views.

These capabilities are critical in user-facing APIs, dashboards, content feeds, and any scenario where your users need to find and sort data dynamically. In the next section, we'll take this even further by looking at **nested resources and custom lookup fields**, so your API supports natural and human-readable URLs even when data relationships get more complex.

Nested Resources and Lookup Fields

In many APIs, resources don't exist in isolation. You often deal with related objects that make sense only in the context of another object. A common example is retrieving all courses created by a specific instructor, or listing all comments that belong to a particular blog post.

These are called **nested resources**—resources that live under or are logically grouped by another parent resource. Nested routing and custom lookup fields allow you to build clean, human-friendly, and meaningful URL structures that reflect the relationship between objects.

In Django REST Framework, you don't have to restructure your models to support this. You only need to handle routing, lookups, and queryset filtering properly.

Scenario: Courses and Modules

Assume you have a `Course` model and a `Module` model. Each module belongs to one course.

```python
# models.py

class Course(models.Model):
    title = models.CharField(max_length=255)
    slug = models.SlugField(unique=True)

class Module(models.Model):
    course = models.ForeignKey(Course,
related_name='modules', on_delete=models.CASCADE)
    title = models.CharField(max_length=255)
```

You want your API to support:

GET `/api/courses/intro-to-django/modules/` — list all modules in the "intro-to-django" course

GET `/api/courses/intro-to-django/modules/5/` — get a specific module in that course

This means using the course slug as the primary identifier, and nesting the module resource under the course.

Step 1: Custom Lookup Fields

By default, DRF uses `pk` (primary key) for lookups. To use a different field like `slug`, set the `lookup_field` in both your viewset and URL patterns.

In your `CourseViewSet`:

```
class CourseViewSet(viewsets.ModelViewSet):
    queryset = Course.objects.all()
    serializer_class = CourseSerializer
    lookup_field = 'slug'
```

Now your endpoint for retrieving a course by slug becomes:

```
GET /api/courses/intro-to-django/
```

Make sure your serializer includes the `slug` field:

```
class
CourseSerializer(serializers.ModelSerializer):
    class Meta:
        model = Course
        fields = ['id', 'title', 'slug']
```

Step 2: Creating a Nested ViewSet

Next, you want a viewset that only shows modules for a specific course. The logic is simple: filter modules based on the `course__slug` parameter captured from the URL.

```
class ModuleViewSet(viewsets.ModelViewSet):
    serializer_class = ModuleSerializer
```

143

```python
    def get_queryset(self):
        course_slug = self.kwargs['course_slug']
        return
Module.objects.filter(course__slug=course_slug)
```

This ensures the list and detail endpoints always return modules that belong to the correct course.

Step 3: Defining Nested Routes

There are two main ways to define nested routes in DRF:

Manually define nested `path()` entries using `urls.py`

Use the `drf-nested-routers` package

Manual Routing

You can write your URLs manually like this:

```python
from django.urls import path
from .views import CourseViewSet, ModuleViewSet

course_list = CourseViewSet.as_view({'get':
'list'})
course_detail = CourseViewSet.as_view({'get':
'retrieve'})
module_list = ModuleViewSet.as_view({'get':
'list'})
module_detail = ModuleViewSet.as_view({'get':
'retrieve'})

urlpatterns = [
    path('courses/', course_list, name='course-
list'),
    path('courses/<slug:slug>/', course_detail,
name='course-detail'),
    path('courses/<slug:course_slug>/modules/',
module_list, name='module-list'),

path('courses/<slug:course_slug>/modules/<int:pk>/'
, module_detail, name='module-detail'),
]
```

This works well and gives you full control.

Using `drf-nested-routers` (Optional)

If you want automatic nested routes, install the package:

```
pip install drf-nested-routers
```

Then set up your routers:

```
from rest_framework_nested.routers import
DefaultRouter, NestedDefaultRouter
from .views import CourseViewSet, ModuleViewSet

router = DefaultRouter()
router.register(r'courses', CourseViewSet,
basename='courses')

courses_router = NestedDefaultRouter(router,
r'courses', lookup='course')
courses_router.register(r'modules', ModuleViewSet,
basename='course-modules')

urlpatterns = router.urls + courses_router.urls
```

This generates routes like:

```
/courses/
```

```
/courses/<slug:slug>/
```

```
/courses/<slug:course_slug>/modules/
```

```
/courses/<slug:course_slug>/modules/<int:pk>/
```

DRF automatically passes the `course_slug` keyword to the `ModuleViewSet`, so your `get_queryset()` method can filter accordingly.

Step 4: Enforcing Ownership or Access Rules

You may want to enforce access control so users can only view or edit nested resources they own. This is where custom permissions and object filtering come in.

For example, if only the instructor should see the modules in their own course:

145

```
def get_queryset(self):
    course_slug = self.kwargs['course_slug']
    return Module.objects.filter(
        course__slug=course_slug,
        course__instructor=self.request.user
    )
```

This prevents unauthorized users from viewing or modifying data they don't own, even if they guess or construct a valid course slug.

Step 5: Custom Lookup Fields in Related Serializers

If you're serializing nested data and want to include a link to the parent resource using a slug instead of an ID, customize the field like this:

```
class
ModuleSerializer(serializers.ModelSerializer):
    course_slug = serializers.SlugRelatedField(
        read_only=True,
        slug_field='slug',
        source='course'
    )

    class Meta:
        model = Module
        fields = ['id', 'title', 'course_slug']
```

This way, every module response contains the slug of its course, making navigation and linking easier on the frontend.

Nested resources and custom lookup fields help you model real-world relationships in a way that is clean, semantic, and intuitive for API consumers. Whether you define your routes manually or use a nested router, the goal is the same: structure your API to reflect the relationships in your data.

To review:

Use `lookup_field = 'slug'` to support clean URLs with slugs instead of IDs

Filter querysets in nested viewsets based on parent parameters (`kwargs`)

Define URLs to reflect the relationship hierarchy

Apply permission checks inside nested views to protect access

Use related fields in serializers to expose readable identifiers

With these techniques in place, your API will be much more usable—especially when consumed by frontend developers, mobile apps, or third-party clients that rely on predictable and meaningful URLs.

Pagination Schemes and Custom Pagination Classes

Once your API starts returning collections of data—courses, users, posts, transactions, or anything else—it becomes essential to break those results into manageable chunks. Without pagination, you risk overwhelming both the client and your backend when datasets grow. Even if you only have a few dozen records today, you're building for scalability, and that means building with pagination from the start.

Django REST Framework includes first-class support for pagination, giving you a few default options as well as the tools to create your own. In this section, we'll cover how DRF pagination works, how to choose the right style, and how to customize it to match your specific frontend or consumer requirements.

Why Pagination Matters

Pagination serves two key purposes:

It prevents returning large payloads that can slow down or crash mobile or low-bandwidth clients.

It gives clients better control over how they consume data—especially in list views, dashboards, or infinite-scroll interfaces.

Even if your database can handle thousands of rows, it doesn't make sense to send them all at once over the network. With proper pagination, you return a small, digestible slice of data along with metadata about how to fetch the next one.

Enabling Pagination in DRF

DRF allows you to set a global pagination style in your settings. You choose one of its built-in pagination classes, then configure the page size and any relevant behavior.

For a traditional numbered pagination setup:

```python
# settings.py

REST_FRAMEWORK = {
    'DEFAULT_PAGINATION_CLASS':
'rest_framework.pagination.PageNumberPagination',
    'PAGE_SIZE': 10
}
```

With this configuration, your paginated list views will respond with a structure like:

```json
{
  "count": 125,
  "next":
"http://localhost:8000/api/courses/?page=2",
  "previous": null,
  "results": [
    {
      "id": 1,
      "title": "Intro to Python",
      "category": "backend"
    },
    ...
  ]
}
```

This format works well for most traditional user interfaces, including HTML pages, data tables, and REST clients.

Pagination Schemes: Available Options

DRF includes three built-in pagination styles. Each is suited for different use cases.

PageNumberPagination

This is the most familiar form—like what you see on blogs or product listings.

```
GET /api/courses/?page=3
```

You can customize the page size per view:

```python
from rest_framework.pagination import
PageNumberPagination

class
SmallPageSizePagination(PageNumberPagination):
    page_size = 5
```

Then in your view:

```python
class CourseViewSet(viewsets.ModelViewSet):
    queryset = Course.objects.all()
    serializer_class = CourseSerializer
    pagination_class = SmallPageSizePagination
```

Clients can also override the page size using a query parameter like `?page_size=20` if you allow it by setting `page_size_query_param` = `'page_size'`.

LimitOffsetPagination

This scheme gives clients more control over the start point and the number of results they want.

```
GET /api/courses/?limit=10&offset=30
```

This request fetches 10 records starting from the 31st (offset is zero-based).

It works well for APIs used by data visualizations or grid components that want precise slicing. Set it like this:

```python
'DEFAULT_PAGINATION_CLASS':
'rest_framework.pagination.LimitOffsetPagination',
```

And optionally configure defaults:

```python
'PAGE_SIZE': 20,
```

The response structure is similar to page-based pagination, but uses `limit` and `offset` instead.

Cursor Pagination

Cursor pagination is designed for large or frequently updated datasets. It avoids the pitfalls of data inconsistency between pages (like items shifting when a new record is added during pagination). It's based on opaque cursors generated from sorting fields.

It supports deep pagination efficiently and works well in time-based feeds or streaming data.

```
GET /api/courses/?cursor=cD0yMDI0LTAzLTIx...
```

Set it like this:

```
'DEFAULT_PAGINATION_CLASS':
'rest_framework.pagination.CursorPagination',
```

And define a default ordering field in your view:

```
class CourseViewSet(viewsets.ModelViewSet):
    ...
    ordering = ['publish_date']
```

Cursor-based pagination requires an unambiguous ordering field—ideally a timestamp or unique value like `created_at` or `id`.

Creating a Custom Pagination Class

If your frontend needs additional metadata, or you want to rename keys in the response, create your own pagination class.

Let's say your frontend team asks for pagination metadata under the key `meta`, and they want the results under `data`.

Here's how you'd write it:

```
from rest_framework.pagination import
PageNumberPagination
from rest_framework.response import Response

class CustomPagination(PageNumberPagination):
    page_size = 10
    page_size_query_param = 'size'
    max_page_size = 100

    def get_paginated_response(self, data):
```

```
        return Response({
            'meta': {
                'total_items':
self.page.paginator.count,
                'total_pages':
self.page.paginator.num_pages,
                'current_page': self.page.number,
                'has_next': self.page.has_next(),
                'has_previous':
self.page.has_previous()
            },
            'data': data
        })
```

Then in your viewset:

```
class CourseViewSet(viewsets.ModelViewSet):
    ...
    pagination_class = CustomPagination
```

The API response now looks like:

```
{
  "meta": {
    "total_items": 84,
    "total_pages": 9,
    "current_page": 1,
    "has_next": true,
    "has_previous": false
  },
  "data": [
    {
      "id": 1,
      "title": "Python for Beginners"
    },
    ...
  ]
}
```

This structure is easier to work with in some frontends, especially when integrating with libraries like Vue, React, or Angular where pagination metadata is expected in a consistent format.

Handling No Pagination

There may be situations where you want to disable pagination entirely—either for a specific endpoint or view.

To disable pagination at the view level:

```
class
AllCoursesViewSet(viewsets.ReadOnlyModelViewSet):
    queryset = Course.objects.all()
    serializer_class = CourseSerializer
    pagination_class = None
```

This tells DRF to return all records without any slicing or metadata. Use this carefully—only in places where the dataset is known to be small and unlikely to grow unbounded.

Best Practices

Always paginate list endpoints, even if your dataset is currently small.

Limit maximum page size to prevent abuse (`max_page_size = 100`).

Choose cursor pagination for real-time feeds or very large datasets.

Use custom pagination classes when your client apps need a specific format.

Combine pagination with filtering, search, and ordering for flexible data access.

Pagination is an essential feature in any real-world API that exposes collections of data. Whether you're listing records for humans, syncing data for mobile apps, or powering visualizations, your consumers need manageable slices of data—along with enough metadata to navigate through them.

With DRF, you can:

Choose between page, offset, and cursor-based schemes

Configure page sizes globally or per view

Customize response structures to match frontend needs

Disable pagination selectively where appropriate

By structuring your paginated responses correctly from the start, you create APIs that scale gracefully and remain easy to consume as your data grows.

Optimizing Database Queries for Performance

If your API endpoints are slow, your users won't care how clean your code is or how many tests you've written. Performance is not a polish step—it's part of building a usable, scalable API. And for Django REST Framework, most of that performance depends on how your queries hit the database.

When you're using Django's ORM through serializers and viewsets, every piece of data fetched is ultimately turned into a SQL query. When things start to slow down, it's almost always because you're issuing too many queries, or you're pulling back too much data per request.

In this section, we'll walk through practical, reliable techniques to optimize your query usage in DRF. You'll learn how to reduce query count with `select_related()` and `prefetch_related()`, how to profile what your views are doing under the hood, and how to avoid common inefficiencies that catch developers off guard.

Understanding the N+1 Query Problem

The most common performance issue in Django APIs is the **N+1 query problem**. This happens when your API fetches a list of objects and, for each one, makes a separate query to fetch related data.

Let's say you're building a course list endpoint, and each course includes its instructor's username.

```python
# serializers.py

class
CourseSerializer(serializers.ModelSerializer):
    instructor_username =
serializers.CharField(source='instructor.username',
read_only=True)
```

```
    class Meta:
        model = Course
        fields = ['id', 'title',
'instructor_username']
```

In your viewset:

```
class CourseViewSet(viewsets.ModelViewSet):
    queryset = Course.objects.all()
```

Even though this looks clean, under the hood it performs:

One query to fetch all courses

One query per course to fetch its instructor

If there are 100 courses, that's 101 queries. This will choke under load.

You can solve this immediately with `select_related()`:

```
queryset =
Course.objects.select_related('instructor')
```

This tells Django to fetch both the course and its instructor in a single SQL JOIN.

Now only **one query** is issued for all courses and their related instructors—no matter how many records are returned.

When to Use `select_related()` VS `prefetch_related()`

They solve similar problems but in different ways.

Use `select_related()` for **foreign key** or **one-to-one** fields.

Use `prefetch_related()` for **many-to-many** or **reverse foreign key** relationships.

For example, if courses have many tags:

```
class Tag(models.Model):
    name = models.CharField(max_length=50)

class Course(models.Model):
    . . .
```

```
    tags = models.ManyToManyField(Tag)
```

And your serializer needs to list them:

```
class
CourseSerializer(serializers.ModelSerializer):
    tags =
serializers.StringRelatedField(many=True)

    class Meta:
        model = Course
        fields = ['id', 'title', 'tags']
```

You should write:

```
queryset = Course.objects.prefetch_related('tags')
```

This results in two queries total:

One for the courses

One for all tags across those courses

Django will then map the tags to the appropriate courses in Python memory—efficient and clean.

If you need both:

```
queryset =
Course.objects.select_related('instructor').prefetc
h_related('tags')
```

Now you're fetching all courses, instructors, and tags with just **three queries**—regardless of the number of courses.

Avoiding Query Explosion in Nested Serializers

Nested serializers are helpful, but they come at a cost if you're not careful.

Suppose you have this:

```
class
InstructorSerializer(serializers.ModelSerializer):
    class Meta:
        model = User
```

```
        fields = ['id', 'username']

class
CourseSerializer(serializers.ModelSerializer):
    instructor =
InstructorSerializer(read_only=True)

    class Meta:
        model = Course
        fields = ['id', 'title', 'instructor']
```

Now every course triggers a full database lookup of the instructor—not just the `username` field. If you haven't used `select_related('instructor')`, you're back to N+1 queries again.

Always inspect your nested relationships and optimize accordingly. If you can use flat serializers (`source='field.subfield'`), use them. If you must use nested serializers, ensure you optimize the queryset behind them.

Monitoring and Debugging Queries

You can't optimize what you can't see. During development, use tools that expose what Django is doing behind the scenes.

The most popular and useful one is **Django Debug Toolbar**:

```
pip install django-debug-toolbar
```

Add it to your `INSTALLED_APPS`, and enable it for local use. It gives you a panel in the browser showing:

The total number of queries per request

Each individual query string

Time taken per query

Which line of code triggered the query

Use this regularly. If you see more than 10 queries for a single list view, inspect your serializers and related fields.

You can also use the Django shell:

```
from django.db import connection
from myapp.models import Course

list(Course.objects.all())  # run your queryset

print(len(connection.queries))  # how many queries
were run
```

This helps you verify whether your queryset is optimized—without needing a browser or frontend.

Using `only()` and `defer()` to Reduce Payload

Sometimes you need to fetch a large number of records but don't need all their fields.

For example, if your API only returns a course's `title` and `slug`, there's no reason to load the `description`, `syllabus`, or `created_at`.

You can limit what fields are selected from the database:

```
Course.objects.only('id', 'title', 'slug')
```

Or skip large fields you know you won't use:

```
Course.objects.defer('description', 'syllabus')
```

This reduces memory usage and speeds up database access, especially with wide tables or rich text fields.

Just make sure your serializer doesn't try to access a field you've deferred— because that would trigger a new query per instance.

Indexing Matters

Sometimes the issue isn't how many queries you make, but how long those queries take to run.

If you're filtering by fields like `slug`, `user_id`, or `created_at`, make sure those fields are indexed:

```
class Course(models.Model):
    slug = models.SlugField(unique=True,
db_index=True)
```

157

Most primary keys and foreign keys are indexed automatically, but any custom filter fields should be reviewed. Use Django migrations to add indexes, and monitor them with your database admin tool (like pgAdmin or MySQL Workbench).

You can also create compound indexes:

```
class Meta:
    indexes = [
        models.Index(fields=['category',
'publish_date']),
    ]
```

This makes multi-column filters perform significantly faster.

Database performance is often the difference between an API that scales and one that stalls. In Django REST Framework, it's easy to write serializers and views that work—but just as easy to create bottlenecks if you don't control what hits the database.

Here's what matters:

Use `select_related()` for foreign key fields to eliminate redundant queries

Use `prefetch_related()` for many-to-many and reverse relations

Use tools like Django Debug Toolbar to audit your query counts

Flatten serializers where possible, and avoid deeply nested relationships unless optimized

Limit fields with `only()` and `defer()` for leaner data pulls

Always index fields you filter or order by

These techniques are not advanced optimizations—they are the baseline for building responsive, production-ready APIs. With them, your endpoints stay fast, even as your data grows.

Now that your API is functionally rich, query-efficient, and properly structured, you're ready to move on to advanced features like **writing nested serializers**, **handling writable relationships**, and designing APIs that don't just read data—but transform and manipulate it safely and correctly.

Chapter 7: Testing and Debugging Your API

Once your API is functionally complete and performant, you need to turn your attention to **confidence**—confidence that what you've built actually works, and that it will continue working as you make changes in the future. That's where testing becomes non-negotiable.

Without automated testing, every change you make introduces uncertainty. You become dependent on manual testing or guesswork. In contrast, with a properly tested API, you can refactor with freedom, add features with certainty, and deploy with peace of mind.

This chapter is your complete guide to testing and debugging Django REST APIs. You'll learn how to write unit and integration tests, use fixtures and factories effectively, mock external dependencies, track test coverage, and make debugging faster with DRF's tools.

Introduction to API Testing Principles

Before writing your first test, it's important to understand why we test APIs in the first place. Testing isn't just about catching bugs—it's about building confidence. You want to know that your endpoints behave consistently, that they return the right data, that they fail gracefully when things go wrong, and that your security controls are actually in place.

An API, by nature, is a contract. It defines how clients can interact with your system—what they can send, what they can expect back, and under what conditions requests will be rejected. When you make changes to your API—whether that's fixing a bug, adding a feature, or refactoring internal code—you need a way to prove that you haven't broken the contract. Testing provides that assurance.

The quality of your tests directly impacts the maintainability and trustworthiness of your application.

The Purpose of Testing in an API Project

When you're working on a Django REST Framework project, testing serves a few specific goals.

First, it verifies that your endpoints behave correctly in response to client input. If a client sends valid data, your API should return the expected response. If they send invalid or incomplete data, the API should reject the request appropriately and return meaningful error information.

Second, it confirms that your **permissions** and **authentication** logic are working as intended. This is particularly important when your views are restricted to certain roles or user states. You don't want a student accessing an admin-only endpoint, or an unauthenticated user modifying resources they shouldn't see.

Third, it validates your **serializers** and **validators**—ensuring that only the right kind of data passes through, and that your database isn't being filled with invalid records.

Lastly, it ensures your application remains **resilient to edge cases** and unexpected inputs. These are the types of errors you often won't catch manually during development. But with a comprehensive test suite, they're easy to reproduce and prevent in the future.

What Should Be Tested?

When building a test strategy for an API, focus on these areas:

Request validation: Do required fields trigger validation errors when missing? Are types enforced? Are custom constraints respected?

Successful responses: Does a `POST` `/api/courses/` return a `201 Created` with the correct structure? Does `GET` `/api/courses/1/` return the right object?

Failure scenarios: What happens if the client tries to create a course with invalid data? Or requests a non-existent resource?

Permissions and authentication: Is access denied where it should be? Are protected endpoints actually protected?

Side effects and business logic: If creating a record triggers an email or updates a related model, does that behavior occur correctly?

To test these areas well, you need different kinds of tests. Django allows you to write tests using `TestCase` or `APITestCase`, but the industry has moved increasingly toward `pytest` because of its cleaner syntax and better plugin ecosystem. Regardless of which tool you choose, the testing principles remain the same.

A Look at a Simple Test

Here's a basic example that tests whether the course list endpoint returns a `200` `OK` status:

```python
# tests/test_courses.py

import pytest
from rest_framework.test import APIClient

@pytest.mark.django_db
def test_course_list_returns_success():
    client = APIClient()
    response = client.get('/api/courses/')
    assert response.status_code == 200
```

This is an **integration test**. It's verifying that the routing, view, serializer, and model are wired together correctly and that the API behaves as expected when a client makes a request.

Now let's say your API requires authentication to create a course. Here's how you'd test that an anonymous user is denied access:

```python
@pytest.mark.django_db
def
test_unauthenticated_user_cannot_create_course():
    client = APIClient()
    payload = {'title': 'Test Course'}
    response = client.post('/api/courses/',
data=payload)
    assert response.status_code == 401  #
Unauthorized
```

In contrast, if an authenticated instructor should be allowed to create a course:

```python
from django.contrib.auth import get_user_model
```

```
from courses.models import Course

User = get_user_model()

@pytest.mark.django_db
def
test_authenticated_instructor_can_create_course():
    user =
User.objects.create_user(username='instructor1',
password='test123', role='instructor')
    client = APIClient()
    client.force_authenticate(user=user)

    payload = {'title': 'Advanced Django REST'}
    response = client.post('/api/courses/',
data=payload)

    assert response.status_code == 201
    assert Course.objects.filter(title='Advanced
Django REST').exists()
```

This test not only checks the HTTP response, but also verifies that the course was actually saved in the database—an important step when testing POST, PUT, or DELETE endpoints.

Making Tests Meaningful

The goal isn't just to get green checks. The goal is to make your API trustworthy. That means your tests should clearly express why a behavior matters.

If you're enforcing a rule that only users with role='instructor' can create courses, write tests that reflect that rule explicitly. If you're sanitizing input or applying transformations, test those behaviors too.

For example, if a course title should be stored in title case:

```
@pytest.mark.django_db
def test_course_title_is_normalized():
    user =
User.objects.create_user(username='instructor',
password='pass', role='instructor')
    client = APIClient()
```

```
    client.force_authenticate(user=user)

    response = client.post('/api/courses/',
data={'title': 'rest api testing'})
    assert response.status_code == 201
    assert response.data['title'] == 'Rest Api
Testing'
```

This kind of test ensures your business rules are preserved—even if a future developer changes the serializer and forgets to apply `.title()`.

Effective testing in an API project comes down to four key ideas:

Test behavior, not implementation. You should be able to change how a view is written without rewriting all your tests. Focus on what the endpoint does from the client's perspective.

Test meaningful paths. Don't just test success—test failure. Think about bad inputs, unauthorized access, or broken assumptions.

Test in isolation where possible. Unit tests help you isolate serializers or custom logic. But integration tests ensure components work together as expected.

Use automation to build trust. A tested API is one you can refactor, deploy, and extend with confidence.

In the rest of this chapter, you'll learn how to write a full suite of unit and integration tests using pytest and Django, how to create reusable test data with factories, how to mock external services, and how to debug issues using real tools—not guesswork. These are the skills that will make your API durable and production-ready.

Unit and Integration Testing with DRF and pytest

When you're building and maintaining an API in Django REST Framework, there are two categories of automated tests that you'll rely on most: **unit tests** and **integration tests**. Both serve different purposes and complement each other.

Unit tests are designed to test individual components of your code in isolation. These might be serializers, validators, model methods, or utilities—things that don't depend on external systems or databases to run correctly.

Integration tests, on the other hand, check how different components interact. These usually involve full HTTP requests hitting your DRF views, checking that authentication, serializers, models, and permissions are all functioning together as expected.

Using **pytest**, which is a popular testing tool in the Python ecosystem, can make both kinds of tests simpler and cleaner to write. It supports function-based tests, automatic fixture discovery, powerful assertions, and plugins that help you test faster and more effectively.

Setting Up `pytest` for Django REST Framework

To get started, install the necessary testing dependencies:

```
pip install pytest pytest-django
```

Then configure pytest by creating a `pytest.ini` file in your project root:

```
[pytest]
```

```
DJANGO_SETTINGS_MODULE = your_project.settings
python_files = tests.py test_*.py *_tests.py
```

This setup allows `pytest` to discover and run your Django tests. You'll also be able to use Django's testing database features seamlessly.

Writing Unit Tests for Serializers

Let's say you have a serializer for a `Course` model:

```python
# serializers.py

class
CourseSerializer(serializers.ModelSerializer):
    class Meta:
        model = Course
        fields = ['title', 'description',
'is_published']
```

You can write a unit test to validate that this serializer accepts valid data and rejects invalid data:

```python
# tests/test_serializers.py

from api.serializers import CourseSerializer

def test_course_serializer_accepts_valid_data():
    data = {
        'title': 'Advanced Django',
        'description': 'Build production-ready
APIs',
        'is_published': True
    }
    serializer = CourseSerializer(data=data)
    assert serializer.is_valid()
    assert serializer.validated_data['title'] ==
'Advanced Django'

def test_course_serializer_rejects_missing_title():
    data = {
        'description': 'Missing title field',
        'is_published': False
    }
    serializer = CourseSerializer(data=data)
    assert not serializer.is_valid()
    assert 'title' in serializer.errors
```

These tests are fast and reliable. They don't depend on a database, and they can be run frequently to validate that your input validation rules remain correct.

Writing Integration Tests for DRF Views

Now let's move from isolated units to full views. These tests simulate actual API calls, including authentication and database interactions. For this, you'll use Django's `APIClient`.

Suppose your API includes a view to list all courses. Here's an integration test that confirms it returns a successful response:

```python
# tests/test_courses.py
```

```python
import pytest
from rest_framework.test import APIClient
from courses.models import Course

@pytest.mark.django_db
def test_course_list_view_returns_200():
    Course.objects.create(title="Python 101",
description="Learn Python", is_published=True)
    client = APIClient()
    response = client.get('/api/courses/')
    assert response.status_code == 200
    assert response.data[0]['title'] == 'Python
101'
```

The `@pytest.mark.django_db` decorator tells pytest this test interacts with the database. That way, you get a fresh test database for each run.

If your endpoint requires authentication, you can authenticate a test user like this:

```python
from django.contrib.auth import get_user_model

User = get_user_model()

@pytest.mark.django_db
def test_authenticated_user_can_create_course():
    user =
User.objects.create_user(username='instructor',
password='pass123', role='instructor')
    client = APIClient()
    client.force_authenticate(user=user)

    data = {'title': 'Test Course', 'description':
'Detailed API course', 'is_published': True}
    response = client.post('/api/courses/',
data=data)

    assert response.status_code == 201
    assert response.data['title'] == 'Test Course'
```

This test checks that an instructor can successfully create a course. It verifies both that the response is correct and that the database has been updated.

Testing Permissions and Access Logic

Testing access control is one of the most important things you can do in an API project. If access rules break, your users might see data they shouldn't— or lose access to features they paid for.

Here's a test to make sure a student cannot create a course:

```
@pytest.mark.django_db
def test_student_cannot_create_course():
    student =
User.objects.create_user(username='learner',
password='1234', role='student')
    client = APIClient()
    client.force_authenticate(user=student)

    response = client.post('/api/courses/',
{'title': 'Invalid', 'description': '...'})

    assert response.status_code == 403  # Forbidden
```

This ensures that your permission classes are properly enforced.

Using Fixtures for Test Data

To avoid repeating setup logic in every test, you can use `pytest` fixtures to create reusable test data:

```
# tests/conftest.py

import pytest
from django.contrib.auth import get_user_model

User = get_user_model()

@pytest.fixture
def instructor():
    return
User.objects.create_user(username='teacher',
password='pass', role='instructor')

@pytest.fixture
def api_client():
```

```
    return APIClient()
```

Then use those fixtures in your tests:

```
@pytest.mark.django_db
def test_authenticated_course_creation(instructor,
api_client):
    api_client.force_authenticate(user=instructor)
    response = api_client.post('/api/courses/', {
        'title': 'Clean Architecture',
        'description': 'Building maintainable
APIs',
        'is_published': True
    })

    assert response.status_code == 201
```

This keeps your tests concise, reduces duplication, and makes your test suite easier to maintain over time.

Organizing Tests for Maintainability

Keep your tests in a directory like tests/, mirroring your app structure:

myproject/

├── **courses/**

│   ├── **models.py**

│   ├── **views.py**

│   └── **serializers.py**

├── **tests/**

│   ├── **test_courses.py**

│   ├── **test_serializers.py**

│   └── **conftest.py**

This way, tests are easy to locate and maintain, especially in a growing codebase. Use descriptive function names that explain what each test is verifying.

Unit and integration tests are your safety net when building and maintaining APIs. Unit tests help you catch logical errors early. Integration tests give you confidence that your endpoints behave as expected in real-world conditions.

Using Django REST Framework with pytest:

Write unit tests for serializers, model methods, and business logic

Write integration tests that hit views through the API client

Use `@pytest.mark.django_db` to safely interact with the test database

Authenticate users using `force_authenticate` to test protected endpoints

Use fixtures to keep your setup logic clean and reusable

With these practices in place, your API becomes reliable, predictable, and easy to change—even years after your first commit. In the next section, we'll take this further by improving test coverage using factories and testing edge cases with reusable fixtures.

Test Coverage, Fixtures, and Factories

When you're writing automated tests for an API, your goal isn't just to write some tests. You want to ensure that your most important logic, security layers, and business rules are covered thoroughly. This is where **test coverage**, **fixtures**, and **factories** come into play.

They each serve different but essential roles:

Coverage gives you visibility into how much of your code is exercised by your test suite.

Fixtures allow you to share setup logic across multiple tests.

Factories generate realistic, dynamic test data quickly, without polluting your tests with hardcoded values.

Together, they help you build a robust and maintainable test suite that supports real development—not just green checkmarks.

Measuring Test Coverage

Test coverage tells you what percentage of your codebase is executed during a test run. It doesn't guarantee quality, but it's a useful signal.

Start by installing `pytest-cov`:

```
pip install pytest-cov
```

Then run your tests with coverage enabled:

```
pytest --cov
```

This will print a summary showing which files were tested and what percentage of their code was executed.

You can also generate an HTML report:

```
pytest --cov --cov-report=html
```

This produces a directory (`htmlcov/`) with a color-coded, line-by-line breakdown of your coverage. Open `htmlcov/index.html` in your browser to see which functions and branches are untested.

For example, you might see that your serializer's `validate_title()` method is never hit in tests. That's your cue to write a test that submits invalid title data and ensures validation works.

Focus your efforts on the most important parts of your application:

Views and endpoints (status codes, data integrity)

Custom permissions

Model methods and constraints

Business logic in serializers and validators

Coverage isn't about hitting 100%. It's about knowing what's tested, what's not, and whether that gap matters.

Using Fixtures to Share Setup Logic

A **fixture** is reusable test setup. When writing multiple tests that depend on the same kind of user, course, or API client, fixtures help you avoid repetition and keep your tests clean.

Create fixtures in a file named `conftest.py` in your `tests/` directory. This file is automatically loaded by `pytest`.

Here's a basic fixture for a user:

```python
# tests/conftest.py

import pytest
from django.contrib.auth import import get_user_model

User = get_user_model()

@pytest.fixture
def instructor_user():
    return
User.objects.create_user(username='instructor',
password='pass', role='instructor')

@pytest.fixture
def api_client():
    from rest_framework.test import APIClient
    return APIClient()
```

You can now use these fixtures in your tests:

```python
@pytest.mark.django_db
def
test_authenticated_course_creation(instructor_user,
api_client):

api_client.force_authenticate(user=instructor_user)

    data = {
        'title': 'REST Best Practices',
        'description': 'Designing clean and secure
APIs',
        'is_published': True
    }

    response = api_client.post('/api/courses/',
data=data)

    assert response.status_code == 201
```

```
assert response.data['title'] == 'REST Best
Practices'
```

Using fixtures reduces cognitive load and repetition. You can refactor your fixtures independently from the tests that use them.

Building Factories with `factory_boy`

Hardcoding test data is fine when you're testing very specific edge cases. But if every test uses the same user data, the same title, or the same email address, you run the risk of test conflicts—or worse, not testing enough variation.

Factories solve this by generating fresh test data dynamically. The `factory_boy` library integrates seamlessly with Django.

First, install the library:

```
pip install factory_boy
```

Now, define a factory for your user model:

```
# tests/factories.py

import factory
from django.contrib.auth import get_user_model
from courses.models import Course

User = get_user_model()

class
UserFactory(factory.django.DjangoModelFactory):
    class Meta:
        model = User

    username = factory.Sequence(lambda n:
f'user{n}')
    email = factory.LazyAttribute(lambda obj:
f'{obj.username}@example.com')
    password =
factory.PostGenerationMethodCall('set_password',
'pass')
    role = 'instructor'
```

```
class
CourseFactory(factory.django.DjangoModelFactory):
    class Meta:
        model = Course

    title = factory.Faker('sentence')
    description = factory.Faker('text')
    is_published = True
    instructor = factory.SubFactory(UserFactory)
```

Now in your tests:

```
@pytest.mark.django_db
def test_course_creation_via_factory(api_client):
    instructor = UserFactory()
    api_client.force_authenticate(user=instructor)

    payload = {
        'title': 'Practical API Testing',
        'description': 'End-to-end strategies for
testing APIs',
        'is_published': True
    }

    response = api_client.post('/api/courses/',
data=payload)
    assert response.status_code == 201
```

Or to create test data before testing retrieval:

```
@pytest.mark.django_db
def
test_course_list_returns_created_courses(api_client
):
    CourseFactory.create_batch(3)
    response = api_client.get('/api/courses/')
    assert response.status_code == 200
    assert len(response.data) == 3
```

Factories allow you to scale your test setup quickly, add variety to your tests, and ensure each test case starts with fresh, realistic data.

Combining Fixtures and Factories

Fixtures and factories work even better together.

Here's how you can create a fixture that returns an authenticated API client:

```python
# tests/conftest.py

@pytest.fixture
def authenticated_client():
    user = UserFactory(role='instructor')
    client = APIClient()
    client.force_authenticate(user=user)
    return client
```

Then in your test:

```python
@pytest.mark.django_db
def
test_authenticated_user_can_see_own_courses(authent
icated_client):
    CourseFactory.create_batch(5)
    response =
authenticated_client.get('/api/courses/')
    assert response.status_code == 200
    assert len(response.data) == 5
```

This approach keeps each test focused, clean, and maintainable.

Automated testing isn't just about writing assertions—it's about building reliable infrastructure to validate your application continuously. Tools like coverage reports, fixtures, and factories make this easier, cleaner, and more effective.

What you've learned here will serve you across your entire project:

Coverage helps you measure what's tested and where to focus next.

Fixtures reduce repetition and keep test setup organized.

Factories generate dynamic, flexible data that improves test realism.

With these in place, you'll be ready to expand your test suite confidently and efficiently. In the next section, we'll talk about mocking—how to isolate your tests from external systems like payment gateways, email providers, or third-party APIs, so you can test business logic without unintended side effects.

Mocking External Dependencies

Not everything your API does happens inside your Django application. In many real-world projects, your views, serializers, or background jobs interact with **external systems**: sending emails, making HTTP requests to third-party APIs, publishing messages to a queue, writing to cloud storage, or charging a user through a payment gateway.

When writing automated tests, you should never rely on real external services. Tests should be **isolated**, **fast**, and **predictable**. Calling actual services makes tests fragile, slow, and dependent on network or third-party reliability.

This is where **mocking** comes in. Mocking allows you to replace external dependencies with controllable, test-safe versions—called "mocks" or "fakes"—that behave predictably and don't produce side effects.

In Python, the standard tool for mocking is `unittest.mock`, which is part of the standard library. Combined with `pytest`, it's a powerful way to keep your tests both safe and meaningful.

When to Mock

Here are situations where mocking is appropriate:

Sending an email using Django's `send_mail` or a third-party email API

Performing an HTTP request using `requests.get()` or `httpx.post()`

Uploading a file to Amazon S3 or another storage provider

Posting a webhook or consuming one

Charging a credit card through Stripe or Paystack

Logging an audit event to an external system

These are **side effects**—actions that affect systems outside your codebase. You don't want your tests to actually perform them. Instead, you mock the function responsible, and assert whether or not it was called, with the expected arguments.

Mocking a Function with `patch`

Suppose you have a service that sends email notifications when a course is published:

```
# services/notifications.py

from django.core.mail import send_mail

def send_course_published_email(course):
    send_mail(
        subject=f"New course published:
{course.title}",
        message="A new course is available.",
        from_email="no-reply@api.com",
        recipient_list=["admin@api.com"]
    )
```

And in your view:

```
# views.py

from services.notifications import
send_course_published_email

class CourseViewSet(viewsets.ModelViewSet):
    ...

    def perform_create(self, serializer):
        course = serializer.save()
        if course.is_published:
            send_course_published_email(course)
```

You want to test this behavior **without sending a real email**. Here's how you mock it:

```
# tests/test_courses.py

from unittest.mock import patch
import pytest
from tests.factories import UserFactory
from rest_framework.test import APIClient
```

```python
@pytest.mark.django_db
@patch('services.notifications.send_course_publishe
d_email')
def
test_email_is_sent_when_course_is_published(mock_se
nd_email):
    user = UserFactory(role='instructor')
    client = APIClient()
    client.force_authenticate(user=user)

    payload = {
        'title': 'Mocking APIs in Python',
        'description': 'An advanced topic',
        'is_published': True
    }

    response = client.post('/api/courses/',
data=payload)

    assert response.status_code == 201
    mock_send_email.assert_called_once()
```

The `@patch()` decorator replaces `send_course_published_email()` with a mock object, which records how it was used. You can now assert:

That it was called

How many times it was called

What arguments were passed

No email is sent. The behavior is tested. The code is safe.

Specifying What a Mock Should Return

Sometimes you want a mocked function to return a specific value. For example, let's say your app posts data to a third-party API and expects a success response.

```python
# services/payment_gateway.py

import requests

def charge_card(token, amount):
```

```
    response =
requests.post("https://api.paygate.com/charge",
json={
        "token": token,
        "amount": amount
    })
    return response.json()
```

To test this without actually hitting the endpoint, you mock `requests.post` and specify what it should return:

```
@patch('services.payment_gateway.requests.post')
def
test_charge_card_returns_expected_data(mock_post):
    mock_post.return_value.json.return_value = {
        "status": "success",
        "transaction_id": "abc123"
    }

    from services.payment_gateway import
charge_card
    result = charge_card(token="tok_test",
amount=5000)

    assert result["status"] == "success"
    assert result["transaction_id"] == "abc123"
```

Here, you control the output of `.json()` even though no real request is made.

This is especially useful when your view logic depends on parsing external responses, and you want to test those branches of logic without relying on live systems.

Mocking with Context Managers

You can also use `patch()` as a context manager instead of a decorator. This is helpful when you only want the mock to apply to part of the test:

```
def test_only_mock_during_this_block():
    with
patch('services.notifications.send_course_published
_email') as mock_email:
        # Call something that triggers email
```

```
    . . .
        assert mock_email.called
```

Once the `with` block exits, the original function is restored.

Mocking with `side_effect`

There are times you want your mock to raise an exception to test error handling. This is done using `side_effect`.

Let's say you want to test what happens when a payment API call fails:

```
@patch('services.payment_gateway.charge_card')
def test_payment_failure(mock_charge):
    mock_charge.side_effect = Exception("Payment
service down")

    client = APIClient()
    user = UserFactory(role='instructor')
    client.force_authenticate(user=user)

    response = client.post('/api/payments/',
{'token': 'abc', 'amount': 1000})

    assert response.status_code == 502  # Your API
handles the error gracefully
```

This test simulates an external failure, helping you validate that your own API responds correctly under pressure.

Structuring Code to Be Mockable

For mocking to work well, your code should **isolate side effects** into dedicated functions or modules. Don't write this:

```
# Avoid
def perform_create(self, serializer):
    data = serializer.save()
    requests.post(...)  # hard to mock cleanly
```

Instead, write:

```
from .services.payment_gateway import charge_card
```

```
def perform_create(self, serializer):
    data = serializer.save()
    charge_card(data.token, data.amount)
```

Now your view calls a function that's easy to patch. This separation of concerns makes your code more testable and easier to maintain.

Mocking external dependencies is one of the most essential techniques in API testing. It allows you to:

Write fast, reliable, and side-effect-free tests

Control external responses to simulate success, failure, or timeout

Test your application's behavior in edge cases without calling real services

Using Python's `unittest.mock`, you can patch any function or object, configure its return values, simulate errors, and inspect how your code uses it—all without leaving the test environment.

Debugging API Issues and Using DRF's Browsable Interface

No matter how carefully you plan your API, at some point you're going to run into unexpected behavior. Maybe an endpoint suddenly returns a 500 error, or the data looks wrong, or your authentication checks aren't working the way they should.

When that happens, your ability to **debug quickly and effectively** becomes critical. You need to trace the source of the problem—whether it's a typo in a serializer, a permission class not firing correctly, a broken query, or a missing migration. And you need the right tools to do it without wasting time on guesswork.

Django REST Framework and Django provide a powerful set of debugging tools that help you do exactly that: identify problems, inspect inputs and outputs, and test behavior directly from your browser without writing temporary scripts or using curl.

Start with the DRF Browsable API

When you run your API in development mode, DRF gives you a browsable web interface for every endpoint.

This interface is more than just a convenience—it's a practical, real-time testing tool.

For any endpoint, it shows:

The serializer schema (what fields are required)

The HTTP methods supported (GET, POST, PUT, PATCH, DELETE)

The structure of the response

Error messages returned by serializers or permissions

Authentication information for the current user

To use it, just run your Django server locally:

```
python manage.py runserver
```

Then visit your API in the browser:

```
http://localhost:8000/api/courses/
```

You'll see a form-like interface where you can submit data, change parameters, and inspect the response structure in real time.

If a request is failing with a 400 or 403 or 500 status code, the browsable API usually shows you **why**—including validation errors, permission issues, or tracebacks (when in debug mode).

This interface lets you:

Test endpoints without Postman or curl

Reproduce bugs quickly by modifying inputs

Try authenticated requests by logging in through the login interface

It is especially helpful for verifying custom serializers, permissions, or nested relationships.

Use Django's Logging for Insights

When things break and you're not sure where or why, good logging is often the fastest path to an answer.

Start by enabling Django's SQL logging in `settings.py`:

```
LOGGING = {
    'version': 1,
    'handlers': {
        'console': {
            'class': 'logging.StreamHandler',
        },
    },
    'loggers': {
        'django.db.backends': {
            'handlers': ['console'],
            'level': 'DEBUG',
        },
    },
}
```

This will print every SQL query Django executes to the console. Useful for:

Checking if a queryset is hitting the database

Verifying whether `select_related` or `prefetch_related` is working

Detecting expensive or redundant queries in list views

If a page is taking longer than expected, SQL logging will often reveal the source.

You can also use logging to trace the execution of your own code:

```
import logging

logger = logging.getLogger(__name__)

def perform_create(self, serializer):
    instance = serializer.save()
    logger.info(f"Created course:
{instance.title}")
```

This log will show up in the console when the endpoint is triggered, giving you live feedback.

Step Through Execution with pdb

When logging isn't enough and you need to look at the exact values being passed around at runtime, use the built-in Python debugger.

Just insert this into any part of your view, serializer, or model logic:

```
import pdb; pdb.set_trace()
```

Then make a request to the endpoint. Your terminal will pause and open an interactive prompt at that line of code.

From here, you can inspect the values of any variables in scope:

```
(pdb) request.user
(pdb) serializer.validated_data
(pdb) course.title
```

You can even step through line by line using:

n (next line)

s (step into)

c (continue execution)

This tool is incredibly useful when debugging logic that is too dynamic or complex to inspect easily with logging alone.

Be sure to remove the pdb lines after you're done—they will block execution if left in your production code.

Using Django Debug Toolbar

If you need deeper insights into your views, especially for performance profiling, install Django Debug Toolbar:

```
pip install django-debug-toolbar
```

Then add it to your INSTALLED_APPS and MIDDLEWARE in settings.py, and hook it into your urls.py.

Once active, you'll see a panel in your browser with:

SQL query counts and durations

Cache usage

Request and response headers

Template rendering stats

Signal usage

Middleware timings

This is ideal for spotting bottlenecks in views, especially when working with large datasets, nested serializers, or complex permissions.

You'll immediately see which queries are being run, how long they take, and whether you've triggered N+1 queries.

Common Pitfalls and Debug Patterns

Silent validation errors

If your serializer is rejecting input and returning a 400 without explanation, inspect `serializer.errors`. DRF always includes a structured explanation in the response body, and the browsable API shows this clearly.

Permission not working as expected

Use `print(request.user)` or `pdb` in your permission class. Often, the issue is that the user is anonymous or lacks the expected role. Also check that your view's `permission_classes` is actually applied—especially if using class inheritance.

Serializer returns empty data

If `serializer.data` is {} or missing fields, check that you're using the correct serializer (read vs. write), and that the instance was saved before serializing. In `create()` or `update()` methods, make sure `return Response(serializer.data)` is not called before saving the object.

Queries not optimized

Use `select_related()` and `prefetch_related()` when accessing related fields in serializers. Use Django Debug Toolbar or SQL logging to verify the number of queries. N+1 problems show up as repeated queries with different IDs.

Debugging is not an emergency process—it's part of how you work day-to-day. The better your tools and habits, the less time you'll waste and the more confidence you'll have in your code.

Here's how to work efficiently with DRF and Django:

Use the **Browsable API** to test requests, inspect payloads, and verify behavior

Use **logging** to see what your application is doing behind the scenes

Use **pdb** to step into live code and inspect variables interactively

Use **Debug Toolbar** to analyze performance, database queries, and request context

These techniques are simple but powerful. They help you diagnose issues quickly, understand your system better, and write cleaner code as a result. With proper testing and effective debugging, you now have a strong foundation for building and maintaining Django REST APIs in production

Chapter 8: Building a Real-World API Project

At this point, you've worked through core concepts, built individual features, and learned how to write, secure, and test Django REST APIs. But knowledge really solidifies when you apply it in the context of a full project—something closer to the complexity of a real application that people would use in production.

In this chapter, we're going to build a practical, fully functional API project from the ground up. You'll see how to translate an idea into an API architecture, model the domain effectively, structure views and workflows, enforce security and validation, and expose a polished, stable API for frontend integration.

You'll not only get code, but a thought process. You'll learn how to think through project architecture, user needs, security trade-offs, and long-term maintainability.

Project Brief: Designing a Real Application (Task Manager)

When you're building APIs professionally, the real work starts before you write a single line of code. It begins with clearly understanding what the application is supposed to do, who's going to use it, and how its pieces should fit together. In a real project, you're not just building endpoints—you're designing workflows, data access rules, and the backend foundation that a frontend or mobile team will trust and rely on.

Let's work through the project brief for a **Task Manager API**—a system where users can organize projects and collaborate by managing tasks.

This project has just the right level of complexity: not trivial, but not so huge that it can't fit in a practical scope. It's something that mirrors what you'd build on the job—whether it's a SaaS tool, internal productivity app, or project management suite.

The Problem We're Solving

Every day, people track work across shared to-do lists, project dashboards, and personal reminders. Developers, designers, writers, and small teams need lightweight ways to manage their tasks. Most of them need to:

Create multiple projects (for different teams or initiatives)

Add and manage tasks inside each project

Assign those tasks to collaborators

Track task status (To Do, In Progress, Done)

Limit access so that users only see their own projects and tasks

You're building an API that powers exactly that. Frontend teams (web or mobile) will use your API to build the user interface. But your job is to get the backend right: accurate, secure, and expressive.

What the API Needs to Do

Let's outline the key responsibilities your API will support:

Authenticated users must be able to create and manage their own **projects**.

A project can contain multiple **tasks**.

Each task can be assigned to a user (either the project owner or other participants).

Tasks must support **statuses** like `"todo"`, `"in_progress"`, and `"done"`.

The API should enforce that users can only see and interact with data they own or are assigned to.

Users should not be able to manipulate others' projects or tasks.

The API should be structured in a way that's easy for frontend teams to consume.

This structure is foundational to how real product teams collaborate. It includes CRUD operations, nested resources, role-specific access, and the kind of validation logic that shows up in production systems.

Thinking Through the Data Structure

You don't want to jump straight into models without considering how things relate. Think of this as a technical blueprint.

A **User** owns multiple **Projects**. A **Project** has multiple **Tasks**. A **Task** might be assigned to a different user. But only users with access to a project can see or interact with its tasks.

You'll need to express those relationships in your models using foreign keys and related names. For example, a `Task` will reference a `Project`, and the `Project` will reference the `User` who owns it.

Let's break it down further by asking the right technical questions:

How do we enforce that only the project owner can create tasks under that project?

How do we make sure a task's `assignee` is a user with access to the project?

How can we allow a frontend to list all tasks in a project, and filter them by status?

Thinking through these kinds of questions before you write your first model or view helps avoid structural mistakes. It also makes the API predictable and easier to integrate with.

Sample Use Case: Jane the Instructor

To make this more concrete, think of Jane, an authenticated user using your app to manage a class she's teaching.

She signs up and logs in. She creates a project called `"Django Bootcamp"` and begins adding tasks like:

```
"Prepare slides"
"Schedule Zoom meeting"
"Review assignments"
```

She sets the status of the first two to `"done"` and `"in_progress"`, assigns one of the tasks to her teaching assistant, and sets due dates for each.

Your API should allow Jane to:

View all her projects

See tasks organized by project

Update task statuses as work progresses

Assign work to specific users (limited to users she collaborates with)

Never access other users' projects or tasks

Every API endpoint you build in this project must support this type of workflow, while keeping everything secure and consistent.

Project Goals and Boundaries

This project won't include a full team management system, notifications, or detailed user roles. The goal is to keep things lean and focused:

Task status management

User-scoped data access

Assigned task relationships

Secure ownership rules

Clean and RESTful endpoints

This is exactly the kind of project that could evolve into a full production app—but here, we're focusing on the foundations.

By the time this API is complete, it will be:

Secure: Every request will be authenticated. Users cannot see or mutate data they don't own.

Structured: The data will be modeled around real-world relationships, and the URL paths will reflect those relationships (e.g., `/projects/5/tasks/`).

Scalable: You'll follow the same patterns you'd use in larger systems, with proper separation of concerns, serializer validation, and permissions.

Frontend-ready: The response format, nested resources, and filtering will make this API easy to integrate with modern frontend frameworks.

This chapter will guide you through every piece—models, serializers, views, permissions, testing, and integration. You won't just build a task manager. You'll walk away with a repeatable blueprint for building professional-grade APIs in Django REST Framework.

Next, we'll start by designing the data models—mapping each real-world entity to a Django model that supports the workflows we've described. Every design decision will be deliberate, grounded in functionality, and implemented with clarity.

Domain Modeling and Architecture

Before you build any feature, endpoint, or authentication flow, you need a solid domain model. That means clearly defining the objects your system will manage, how those objects relate to each other, and which user actions are allowed or restricted for each relationship.

This is where a lot of APIs go wrong. If you don't get your models and architecture right, you'll end up patching over design flaws later with custom logic, redundant serializers, or complicated view logic that tries to compensate for poor structure. But when your models reflect your real business rules, everything downstream becomes easier: validation, permissions, testing, and even documentation.

Let's take the project brief from earlier and now turn that into a well-structured Django backend.

Identifying the Entities

Based on the task manager application you're building, there are three primary domain entities you'll be working with:

`User` (provided by Django's auth system)

`Project` (created and owned by a user)

`Task` (attached to a project, optionally assigned to a user)

You're also going to need to enforce access rules, track task status, and support features like task filtering and ownership enforcement. All of that starts with a clean database schema and relationship modeling.

Defining the Data Model with Django ORM

Let's begin with the `Project` model. Each project belongs to a user, which you'll refer to as the owner. A project can have many tasks.

```python
# tasks/models.py

from django.db import models
from django.contrib.auth import get_user_model

User = get_user_model()

class Project(models.Model):
    name = models.CharField(max_length=100)
    description = models.TextField(blank=True)
    owner = models.ForeignKey(User,
on_delete=models.CASCADE, related_name='projects')
    created_at =
models.DateTimeField(auto_now_add=True)

    def __str__(self):
        return self.name
```

The `related_name='projects'` allows you to access all projects for a user using `user.projects.all()`. This becomes especially useful when building queries or permission checks later on.

Next is the `Task` model. Each task is part of a project and can optionally be assigned to a user (who must be someone involved in the project). The task also has a status field and other metadata.

```python
class Task(models.Model):
    STATUS_CHOICES = [
        ('todo', 'To Do'),
        ('in_progress', 'In Progress'),
        ('done', 'Done'),
    ]
```

```
    title = models.CharField(max_length=100)
    description = models.TextField(blank=True)
    project = models.ForeignKey(Project,
on_delete=models.CASCADE, related_name='tasks')
    assignee = models.ForeignKey(User,
on_delete=models.SET_NULL, null=True, blank=True)
    status = models.CharField(max_length=20,
choices=STATUS_CHOICES, default='todo')
    due_date = models.DateField(null=True,
blank=True)
    created_at =
models.DateTimeField(auto_now_add=True)

    def __str__(self):
        return self.title
```

This model structure supports the core relationships your system needs:

A user owns a project

A project has many tasks

A task may or may not have an assignee

A task belongs to one project

You've also included a simple but extensible status system using `choices`, which DRF handles gracefully when validating data.

Data Integrity and Relational Constraints

Your database should enforce the constraints your application logic expects.

When a project is deleted, all its tasks should also be deleted. This is already handled because the `project` field uses `on_delete=models.CASCADE`.

When a user is deleted, you likely don't want to delete all tasks they were assigned to—but you do want those tasks to remain in the system. That's why `assignee` uses `on_delete=models.SET_NULL` instead of `CASCADE`.

You've also allowed `assignee` to be `null`, because not every task is assigned when it's created. You might assign tasks later.

Structuring Relationships for Query Efficiency

A major benefit of thinking carefully through your models is that you can then write efficient, readable queries with no custom SQL. For example:

All tasks for a given project:

```
project.tasks.all()
```

All tasks assigned to a user:

```
Task.objects.filter(assignee=user)
```

All tasks that are due tomorrow and are still in progress:

```
Task.objects.filter(status='in_progress',
due_date=datetime.date.today() + timedelta(days=1))
```

All projects owned by a user:

```
user.projects.all()
```

These kinds of queries will power your API views, serializers, and filters. By modeling your domain clearly from the start, these queries stay simple and safe to use.

Structuring the Project Itself

Your Django project should follow a modular structure that separates your API logic into manageable pieces:

taskmanager/

├── manage.py

├── taskmanager/   **← project settings**

| └── settings.py

├── users/   **← custom user logic, if needed**

├── tasks/   **← models, views, serializers for the task manager**

| ├── models.py

| ├── serializers.py

```
|     ├── views.py
|     ├── permissions.py
|     ├── urls.py
|     └── tests/
```

Later, when you begin exposing nested views (like `/projects/3/tasks/`), the separation of apps and routes will help keep your project maintainable. Each domain concern—authentication, task tracking, admin tools—can live in its own module without becoming tangled.

Domain Rules That Will Inform Your API Logic

Your models encode structure, but the actual rules you enforce will live in serializers, permissions, and views. Some of those rules, which you'll enforce later, include:

A user cannot view or create a task on a project they don't own

A task's assignee must be a valid user (and optionally part of the project)

Task status must always be one of the predefined values

Task due dates should not be set in the past (this is optional, but a good rule)

These rules map directly to validation logic and permission classes. The more your models reflect reality, the simpler these rules become to write and test.

Your domain model is the foundation of everything that follows. When you clearly express your relationships and constraints in your Django models, you prevent problems later in your views, serializers, and business logic.

With the models in place, you're now ready to begin building out the core features—creating projects, managing tasks, and enforcing security through serializers and views. The next section will guide you through implementing those features, from endpoint structure to business logic.

Building Core Features and Workflows

Now that your domain model is defined, it's time to build out the core features of the API that make it usable: creating projects, managing tasks within those projects, assigning work to other users, and enforcing clear access rules.

This is where your API goes from being a schema to something interactive—where users can perform meaningful actions through clean, predictable HTTP endpoints. The goal is to build workflows that align with how real users would interact with a system like this: from creating a new project to tracking the status of their tasks.

Everything here will be implemented with Django REST Framework's serializers, viewsets, and routers. You'll ensure each feature is structured, secure, and testable.

Project Creation and Ownership Enforcement

The `Project` model is owned by a user. This means when a project is created, it must be automatically linked to the authenticated user making the request.

Start with the serializer:

```python
# tasks/serializers.py

from rest_framework import serializers
from .models import Project

class
ProjectSerializer(serializers.ModelSerializer):
    class Meta:
        model = Project
        fields = ['id', 'name', 'description',
'created_at']
        read_only_fields = ['id', 'created_at']
```

This serializer exposes just the necessary fields. You'll attach the `owner` in the view, not from the incoming request data.

Now the viewset:

```python
# tasks/views.py

from rest_framework import viewsets, permissions
from .models import Project
from .serializers import ProjectSerializer

class ProjectViewSet(viewsets.ModelViewSet):
    serializer_class = ProjectSerializer
    permission_classes =
[permissions.IsAuthenticated]

    def get_queryset(self):
        return
Project.objects.filter(owner=self.request.user)

    def perform_create(self, serializer):
        serializer.save(owner=self.request.user)
```

By overriding `get_queryset`, you're enforcing that users only see their own projects. The `perform_create()` method attaches the authenticated user as the project owner during save.

Listing and Creating Tasks Within Projects

Each task belongs to a project. When creating a task, the user must specify which project it belongs to—and that project must belong to them.

Start with the serializer:

```python
# tasks/serializers.py

from .models import Task

class TaskSerializer(serializers.ModelSerializer):
    assignee_username =
serializers.CharField(source='assignee.username',
read_only=True)

    class Meta:
        model = Task
        fields = [
            'id', 'title', 'description', 'status',
```

```
             'due_date', 'project', 'assignee',
'assignee_username',
             'created_at'
        ]
        read_only_fields = ['id', 'created_at',
'assignee_username']

    def validate_project(self, project):
        user = self.context['request'].user
        if project.owner != user:
            raise serializers.ValidationError("You
do not own this project.")
        return project
```

This ensures a user cannot attach a task to someone else's project. You're checking that the authenticated user is the owner of the `project` passed in the request.

Next, the view:

```
class TaskViewSet(viewsets.ModelViewSet):
    serializer_class = TaskSerializer
    permission_classes =
[permissions.IsAuthenticated]

    def get_queryset(self):
        return
Task.objects.filter(project__owner=self.request.use
r)
```

This ensures users can only read tasks that belong to their projects. It doesn't matter which project ID is passed in—this filter will prevent unauthorized access.

At this point, users can:

Create tasks under their own projects

Assign them to any user (we'll add further constraints later)

View tasks filtered by project ownership

Supporting Task Assignment Workflows

In a real-world project manager, you may want to assign tasks to collaborators. For now, we'll allow a task to be assigned to any valid user, but still enforce project ownership.

Later on, you might add support for project members or teams—but for this version, only the project owner can assign tasks.

This is enforced in the `validate_assignee()` method:

```
def validate_assignee(self, user):
    request = self.context['request']
    project = self.initial_data.get('project')

    if not project:
        raise serializers.ValidationError("Project
is required before assigning a user.")

    from .models import Project
    project_obj =
Project.objects.filter(id=project,
owner=request.user).first()

    if not project_obj:
        raise serializers.ValidationError("You do
not own the specified project.")

    return user
```

This prevents someone from assigning a task to another user on a project they don't own. You're checking the project exists and is owned by the current user before allowing assignment.

Status Updates and Task Progression

Task progression is a fundamental workflow. The frontend might show a kanban board with columns for "To Do," "In Progress," and "Done."

Because `status` is modeled as a choice field, DRF will automatically enforce that only allowed values can be submitted:

```
status = models.CharField(max_length=20, choices=[
    ('todo', 'To Do'),
    ('in_progress', 'In Progress'),
```

```
        ('done', 'Done'),
])
```

So if a user submits `status='completed'`, the serializer will reject the request with a 400 response.

Here's how a frontend might send a PATCH request:

```
PATCH /api/tasks/12/
Content-Type: application/json

{
   "status": "in_progress"
}
```

And your API will validate and save it—no additional code required unless you want to customize transitions or rules for who can change status.

Secure Filtering and Pagination

As your data grows, the frontend needs ways to request only specific results—tasks by project, tasks due today, tasks still pending.

DRF supports this through filtering and pagination. You can enable this in `settings.py`:

```
REST_FRAMEWORK = {
    'DEFAULT_FILTER_BACKENDS':
['django_filters.rest_framework.DjangoFilterBackend
'],
    'DEFAULT_PAGINATION_CLASS':
'rest_framework.pagination.PageNumberPagination',
    'PAGE_SIZE': 10
}
```

Install Django Filter if you haven't already:

```
pip install django-filter
```

Then add filters to your view:

```
from django_filters.rest_framework import
DjangoFilterBackend
from rest_framework import filters
```

```
class TaskViewSet(viewsets.ModelViewSet):
    ...
    filter_backends = [DjangoFilterBackend,
filters.OrderingFilter, filters.SearchFilter]
    filterset_fields = ['status', 'project',
'assignee']
    ordering_fields = ['due_date', 'created_at']
    search_fields = ['title', 'description']
```

Now your API supports queries like:

```
GET /api/tasks/?status=todo&project=3
GET /api/tasks/?search=meeting
GET /api/tasks/?ordering=due_date
```

You've enabled real, dynamic workflows with minimal effort.

With these core features in place, your API now allows users to:

Create and manage projects securely

Add, update, and delete tasks within those projects

Assign tasks to users under strict project ownership rules

Track task statuses and sort or search based on their fields

Interact with a structure that's clean, reliable, and secure

All of this was achieved with DRF's standard tools—ModelViewSets, serializers, and permission logic. You didn't need to reach for complex patterns or custom endpoints. The strength of DRF lies in this kind of structure: consistent, predictable, and extendable.

Securing, Validating, and Testing the Project

Once your API can handle core workflows—creating projects, assigning tasks, updating status—the next priority is to secure it. Functional APIs that aren't properly validated or protected are liabilities. You must ensure every action is authenticated, every request is validated, and every endpoint behaves exactly as it should, even when used incorrectly or maliciously.

Security, validation, and testing work together. Security ensures the wrong users can't do the wrong things. Validation ensures that even the right users can't provide bad input. Testing ensures everything behaves as expected, every time—even after changes or refactors.

Enforcing Authentication and Global Permissions

By default, DRF allows unrestricted access unless you configure it otherwise. For a task management API, this is unacceptable. Every single request— whether it's for listing tasks, updating a project, or assigning users—must be made by an authenticated user.

In `settings.py`, define your default permission and authentication classes:

```
# settings.py

REST_FRAMEWORK = {
    'DEFAULT_AUTHENTICATION_CLASSES': [

'rest_framework.authentication.TokenAuthentication'
'
    ],
    'DEFAULT_PERMISSION_CLASSES': [

'rest_framework.permissions.IsAuthenticated',
    ],
}
```

This enforces that **every endpoint** requires a valid token. Any unauthenticated request will receive a `401 Unauthorized` response.

Now install token auth if it hasn't been added yet:

```
pip install djangorestframework
```

Then add `'rest_framework.authtoken'` to your INSTALLED_APPS and run migrations:

```
python manage.py migrate
```

To create tokens on user login, you can wire up a login view using DRF's built-in token view or implement a custom one using JWT.

Example using the built-in token view:

```
from rest_framework.authtoken.views import
obtain_auth_token
from django.urls import path

urlpatterns = [
    path('api/token/', obtain_auth_token),
]
```

Now, every authenticated request must include a token in the header:

```
Authorization: Token abc123xyz456
```

Securing Access to Data: Custom Permissions

Beyond simple authentication, users must only access data they own or are permitted to view.

You've already written filters in your viewsets to limit querysets:

```
def get_queryset(self):
    return
Project.objects.filter(owner=self.request.user)
```

But this is not enough for object-level access. DRF lets users override get_queryset() to control list access, but individual object access—like GET /projects/5/—requires a **permission class** to validate the object belongs to the user.

Here's how to enforce object-level permissions:

```
# tasks/permissions.py

from rest_framework import permissions

class IsProjectOwner(permissions.BasePermission):
    def has_object_permission(self, request, view,
obj):
        return obj.owner == request.user
```

Now apply this to your ProjectViewSet:

```
from .permissions import IsProjectOwner
```

```
class ProjectViewSet(viewsets.ModelViewSet):
    ...

    permission_classes =
[permissions.IsAuthenticated, IsProjectOwner]
```

This ensures that even if a user guesses a project ID, they won't be able to read, update, or delete it unless they own it.

You can do something similar for tasks:

```
class IsTaskOwner(permissions.BasePermission):
    def has_object_permission(self, request, view,
obj):
        return obj.project.owner == request.user
```

Always think in terms of **ownership hierarchy**. A task doesn't belong directly to a user—it belongs to a project, and that project has an owner. Your permissions should reflect that structure.

Validating Data Properly in Serializers

Validation is your first line of defense against corrupted, invalid, or malicious data. DRF gives you fine-grained control over how fields are validated.

Let's say you want to ensure that task due dates are not in the past. Add a custom validator to your serializer:

```
from datetime import date
from rest_framework import serializers

class TaskSerializer(serializers.ModelSerializer):
    ...

    def validate_due_date(self, value):
        if value and value < date.today():
            raise serializers.ValidationError("Due
date cannot be in the past.")
        return value
```

You've already validated that users can't attach tasks to other people's projects, but you can refine that too:

```
def validate_project(self, project):
    if project.owner !=
self.context['request'].user:
        raise serializers.ValidationError("You do
not own this project.")
    return project
```

This enforces clean data at the boundary of your system—before it even hits your database or view logic.

Validation should never be treated as optional. It ensures your system stays consistent and defensible under real usage.

Writing Tests with pytest and DRF Test Client

With security and validation in place, it's time to test it.

First, install the required packages if not done already:

```
pip install pytest pytest-django
```

Configure `pytest.ini`:

```
[pytest]
DJANGO_SETTINGS_MODULE = your_project.settings
python_files = tests.py test_*.py *_tests.py
```

Let's write a test to ensure a user cannot access another user's project:

```
# tests/test_project_permissions.py

import pytest
from rest_framework.test import APIClient
from django.contrib.auth import get_user_model
from tasks.models import Project

User = get_user_model()

@pytest.mark.django_db
def test_user_cannot_access_others_project():
    owner =
User.objects.create_user(username='owner',
password='pass')
```

```python
    intruder =
User.objects.create_user(username='intruder',
password='pass')

    project = Project.objects.create(name="Private
Project", owner=owner)

    client = APIClient()
    client.force_authenticate(user=intruder)

    response =
client.get(f'/api/projects/{project.id}/')
    assert response.status_code == 403
```

Now a test for invalid task due dates:

```python
from datetime import timedelta, date
from tasks.models import Task, Project

@pytest.mark.django_db
def test_task_cannot_have_due_date_in_past():
    user =
User.objects.create_user(username='testuser',
password='testpass')
    project = Project.objects.create(name="Test
Project", owner=user)

    client = APIClient()
    client.force_authenticate(user=user)

    past_date = date.today() - timedelta(days=1)

    response = client.post('/api/tasks/', {
        'title': 'Past Task',
        'status': 'todo',
        'due_date': past_date,
        'project': project.id
    })

    assert response.status_code == 400
    assert 'due_date' in response.data
```

These tests aren't just about code correctness—they protect business rules and ensure your API remains consistent and secure.

At this point in your project, you've gone beyond just building features. You've made the API robust—resistant to abuse, bad input, and unauthorized access. You've also built a foundation for trust—because your tests prove that your business rules are being enforced correctly.

Here's what's now part of your system:

Every endpoint requires a valid authentication token

All project and task data is access-controlled based on the user

Custom permission classes enforce object-level protection

Serializer validation prevents invalid assignments or broken task rules

Unit and integration tests confirm that core security and workflow rules hold

This is the kind of engineering discipline that makes APIs production-worthy—not just working, but reliable. The next step is to open it up to the outside world. In the final section of this chapter, you'll expose your API for frontend integration—ensuring your endpoints are clean, discoverable, and easy to work with across web, mobile, or third-party clients.

Exposing the API for Frontend Consumption

After you've secured your endpoints, validated your data, and built reliable workflows, the next step is to prepare your API for real-world consumption. Whether it's a frontend team working in Vue or React, a mobile app making network calls from Swift or Kotlin, or even a third-party integrator consuming your endpoints via token authentication, the goal is the same: your API must be clear, consistent, and reliable.

What makes an API "consumable" isn't just whether it technically returns JSON. It's about whether other developers—ones who don't have your models, your database access, or your assumptions—can understand how to interact with it safely and predictably.

This section focuses on making your Django REST API frontend-ready. You'll configure CORS, polish your response formats, provide filtering and pagination, and optionally expose Swagger documentation to make your endpoints self-describing.

Enabling Cross-Origin Requests (CORS)

Most frontend applications run on a different origin than your backend API. If your frontend is hosted at `https://frontend-client.com` and your API runs at `https://api.server.com`, browsers will block requests unless your server explicitly allows them. That's what CORS is for.

To allow cross-origin requests, install the CORS middleware:

```
pip install django-cors-headers
```

Then update your `settings.py`:

```
INSTALLED_APPS += ['corsheaders']

MIDDLEWARE =
['corsheaders.middleware.CorsMiddleware'] +
MIDDLEWARE

CORS_ALLOW_ALL_ORIGINS = True   # For development
only!
```

During production, always restrict it to known, trusted domains:

```
CORS_ALLOWED_ORIGINS = [
    "https://frontend-client.com",
    "http://localhost:3000"
]
```

This allows frontend apps—whether local or deployed—to interact with your API using AJAX, fetch, or Axios.

Structuring Endpoints for Predictability

The frontend team shouldn't have to guess how to access project data or how to assign a task. Your endpoints should follow consistent, predictable REST conventions.

Using Django REST Framework's routers and viewsets, you get clean URLs automatically:

```
GET       /api/projects/              → list all user-owned
projects

POST      /api/projects/              → create a new project

GET       /api/projects/4/            → retrieve one project

PUT       /api/projects/4/            → update a project

DELETE    /api/projects/4/            → delete a project


GET       /api/tasks/                 → list all tasks user
has access to

POST      /api/tasks/                 → create a task

GET       /api/tasks/10/              → get a specific task

PATCH     /api/tasks/10/              → update task status
or assignment
```

If your frontend needs nested data (for example, all tasks under a specific project), DRF makes that easy with query parameters:

```
GET /api/tasks/?project=4
```

This avoids needing a special /projects/4/tasks/ endpoint, and gives frontend developers full control over filtering.

Providing Filtering, Ordering, and Pagination

A good API supports both **precision** and **scalability**. That means letting the frontend get only what it needs (e.g., incomplete tasks due today) without returning thousands of rows.

Use DRF's built-in support for filtering, searching, and pagination:

1. Pagination

In settings.py:

```
REST_FRAMEWORK = {
```

```
    'DEFAULT_PAGINATION_CLASS':
'rest_framework.pagination.PageNumberPagination',
    'PAGE_SIZE': 10
}
```

All list endpoints will now return data like:

```
{
  "count": 42,
  "next":
"http://api.example.com/api/tasks/?page=2",
  "previous": null,
  "results": [
    {
      "id": 1,
      "title": "Write test coverage",
      ...
    }
  ]
}
```

This structure is easy to paginate from a frontend using infinite scroll, "Load More" buttons, or traditional pagination controls.

2. Filtering and Ordering

Add filters to your `TaskViewSet`:

```
from django_filters.rest_framework import
DjangoFilterBackend
from rest_framework import filters

class TaskViewSet(viewsets.ModelViewSet):
    ...
    filter_backends = [DjangoFilterBackend,
filters.OrderingFilter, filters.SearchFilter]
    filterset_fields = ['status', 'project',
'assignee']
    ordering_fields = ['created_at', 'due_date']
    search_fields = ['title', 'description']
```

Now frontend developers can fetch exactly what they need:

```
GET
/api/tasks/?status=in_progress&ordering=due_date
GET /api/tasks/?search=meeting
```

They won't need any backend changes to add new filters—they can just use the querystring interface.

Flattening and Simplifying Responses

DRF serializers already produce JSON, but you want to make sure your API responses are:

Easy to work with from JavaScript

Explicit (no hidden relationships)

Free from redundant nesting

For instance, in your `TaskSerializer`, expose useful data that avoids extra requests:

```
class TaskSerializer(serializers.ModelSerializer):
    assignee_username =
serializers.CharField(source='assignee.username',
read_only=True)

    class Meta:
        model = Task
        fields = [
            'id', 'title', 'description', 'status',
            'due_date', 'assignee',
'assignee_username',
            'project', 'created_at'
        ]
```

Now your frontend can show:

```
{
  "id": 12,
  "title": "Deploy production build",
  "assignee": 4,
  "assignee_username": "janedoe",
  "status": "done"
}
```

The `assignee` gives you the ID for future API calls. The `assignee_username` lets you display meaningful labels immediately.

Avoid deeply nested JSON unless absolutely necessary. Flat, reference-based data is easier to render and cache.

Authenticating from the Frontend

If your frontend is a Single Page App (SPA) or mobile app, it will authenticate using a login endpoint that returns a token.

Here's how a Vue or React frontend would authenticate:

```
POST /api/token/
{
    "username": "janedoe",
    "password": "securepass"
}
```

The backend responds with:

```
{
    "token": "abc123xyz456"
}
```

Subsequent requests must include:

```
Authorization: Token abc123xyz456
```

The frontend should store this token securely—typically in memory for SPAs, or in secure storage for mobile apps. Never store tokens in `localStorage` if you're concerned about XSS vulnerabilities.

Auto-Generating API Documentation

Even if your frontend team works closely with you, self-documenting APIs reduce friction and prevent back-and-forth.

Use `drf-spectacular` to generate an OpenAPI/Swagger schema:

```
pip install drf-spectacular
```

In `settings.py`:

```
REST_FRAMEWORK['DEFAULT_SCHEMA_CLASS'] =
'drf_spectacular.openapi.AutoSchema'
```

Then expose schema and Swagger docs in `urls.py`:

```
from drf_spectacular.views import
SpectacularAPIView, SpectacularSwaggerView

urlpatterns = [
    path('api/schema/',
SpectacularAPIView.as_view(), name='schema'),
    path('api/docs/',
SpectacularSwaggerView.as_view(url_name='schema'),
name='swagger-ui'),
]
```

Now any developer can open `/api/docs/` in a browser and see all endpoints, parameters, request bodies, and expected responses—automatically generated from your serializers and views.

You've now made your API truly usable—not just internally, but externally by other developers, frontend teams, and third-party integrators.

Here's what's now part of your frontend-facing API strategy:

Cross-origin support via CORS

RESTful, predictable URLs and methods

Filtering, searching, and pagination built-in

Flat, useful JSON responses

Auth via token-based login

Auto-generated, browsable Swagger docs

With these capabilities in place, you're not just building endpoints—you're providing a backend service that's scalable, predictable, and a pleasure to work with.

Chapter 9: Preparing for Production

You've now built a fully functioning, secure, and validated Django REST API. You've defined your domain logic clearly, written clean endpoints, enforced permissions, and tested everything carefully. At this point, you're ready to move beyond your development environment and start thinking about production.

Shipping an API into production is more than pushing your code to a server. It's about setting up a secure, stable, scalable environment where your application can run reliably—without breaking under load, leaking data, or failing silently when something goes wrong.

In this chapter, you'll learn how to configure Django for a production environment, manage static files and uploads, log and monitor your application, package it with Docker, and deploy it using a reliable combination of **Gunicorn**, **Nginx**, and **PostgreSQL**.

Production Settings and Environment Variables

Once your Django REST API is functionally complete and tested, one of the most critical steps before deployment is ensuring that your application settings are production-safe. Development settings are intentionally permissive and insecure—they're designed to make it easy to test and debug locally. But running your API in production with `DEBUG=True`, a hardcoded `SECRET_KEY`, or unrestricted CORS is an open invitation for problems.

What you need is a clean separation between development and production configurations, and a secure way to manage sensitive values like database URLs, secret keys, and API tokens. That's what this section will help you do.

Separating Settings by Environment

In development, you want full access to debugging tools and automatic static file serving. In production, you want those things disabled. Django makes it easy to split settings by environment using multiple settings files.

Instead of putting all your settings in `settings.py`, you can restructure them like this:

your_project/

├── settings/

│ ├── __init__.py

│ ├── base.py

│ ├── development.py

│ └── production.py

Your `base.py` contains settings common to all environments: installed apps, middleware, templates, etc. Then in `development.py` and `production.py`, you import from `base` and override what's specific.

Here's a minimal `production.py`:

```python
# your_project/settings/production.py

from .base import *
import os

DEBUG = False

ALLOWED_HOSTS = ['api.yourdomain.com']

SECRET_KEY = os.environ.get('DJANGO_SECRET_KEY')

CSRF_TRUSTED_ORIGINS =
['https://api.yourdomain.com']

SECURE_HSTS_SECONDS = 31536000
SECURE_SSL_REDIRECT = True
SESSION_COOKIE_SECURE = True
CSRF_COOKIE_SECURE = True
```

With these settings, you've:

Turned off debug mode

Whitelisted your production domain

Loaded your secret key securely from the environment

Enforced HTTPS-only cookies and redirection

Enabled HTTP Strict Transport Security (HSTS)

You'll use DJANGO_SETTINGS_MODULE to select which settings file to use when deploying:

```
DJANGO_SETTINGS_MODULE=your_project.settings.produc
tion
```

Using Environment Variables for Secrets and Config

Hardcoding credentials, API keys, or URLs directly in your settings file is a dangerous practice. If your code is pushed to a public repository or a shared server, those secrets can leak—and they often do.

A much safer and more flexible approach is to use **environment variables**.

Django won't read .env files by itself, so the best way to work with them is by using django-environ. It provides a clean way to read typed values from environment variables.

Install the package:

```
pip install django-environ
```

Now update your base.py settings file:

```
import environ
import os

env = environ.Env()

# Load .env file if it exists
environ.Env.read_env(os.path.join(BASE_DIR,
'.env'))
```

```
SECRET_KEY = env('DJANGO_SECRET_KEY')

DEBUG = env.bool('DJANGO_DEBUG', default=False)

ALLOWED_HOSTS = env.list('DJANGO_ALLOWED_HOSTS',
default=[])
```

Now you can create a .env file locally for development:

```
DJANGO_SECRET_KEY=dev-unsafe-key
DJANGO_DEBUG=True
DJANGO_ALLOWED_HOSTS=localhost,127.0.0.1
```

And on your production server, set environment variables using your process manager, Docker environment, or cloud service configuration panel—never store the .env file directly on the server if it contains sensitive values.

This allows you to change deployment details—like the database or email service—without ever touching your source code.

Managing the Database URL

Instead of manually defining the database dictionary, you can also load it directly from an environment variable:

```
DATABASES = {
    'default': env.db('DATABASE_URL')
}
```

Set this in your environment:

```
DATABASE_URL=postgres://user:password@host:5432/dbn
ame
```

Now your entire database connection (driver, credentials, host, port, database name) is abstracted into a single, secure variable—easy to change per environment.

Recommended Production Settings to Enforce

In addition to basic security flags and secrets, you should configure the following for production:

```
# production.py
```

```
SECURE_HSTS_SECONDS = 31536000  # Enforce HTTPS for
1 year
SECURE_BROWSER_XSS_FILTER = True
SECURE_CONTENT_TYPE_NOSNIFF = True

X_FRAME_OPTIONS = 'DENY'
SESSION_COOKIE_SECURE = True
CSRF_COOKIE_SECURE = True

DEFAULT_AUTO_FIELD =
'django.db.models.BigAutoField'
```

These settings:

Prevent the site from being framed (clickjacking)

Force cookies to only be sent over HTTPS

Help protect against XSS and content sniffing

Reduce the chance of accidental schema collisions in future migrations

None of these settings will break your site—but they will protect it in subtle but critical ways.

Switching Between Environments

You can now launch Django with the appropriate settings module using the environment variable:

```
DJANGO_SETTINGS_MODULE=your_project.settings.produc
tion python manage.py migrate
DJANGO_SETTINGS_MODULE=your_project.settings.produc
tion gunicorn your_project.wsgi:application
```

In local development, you might use:

```
DJANGO_SETTINGS_MODULE=your_project.settings.develo
pment python manage.py runserver
```

Or set the default in your .env:

```
DJANGO_SETTINGS_MODULE=your_project.settings.produc
tion
```

This clean separation makes deployments safer, reduces the risk of configuration drift, and allows you to audit your settings with confidence.

This isn't just about making your code work in production—it's about making it **safe**, **maintainable**, and **easily configurable** across environments.

What you've done here is fundamental to a professional-grade Django API:

Moved sensitive values like secret keys and database credentials out of source code

Split development and production settings for clarity and control

Enforced security best practices with HTTPS, CSRF protection, and secure cookies

Used `django-environ` to read typed values from `.env` files or shell environments

Structured your API so it can be reliably deployed with the correct config every time

Everything else in your production pipeline—deployment tools, Docker containers, CI/CD systems—will depend on the foundation you've just laid. If your settings are clean and environment-driven, your API will remain predictable and safe regardless of where or how it runs.

Static Files, Media, and File Uploads

When you're running a Django REST API in development, things often seem deceptively simple. Static files work without any configuration. File uploads just land in your local file system. But in production, you don't have those conveniences. You have to deliberately configure how static assets are collected, where uploaded files go, and how both are served to clients—without blocking or overloading your Django process.

In Django, **static files** are assets that are part of your application—CSS files, JavaScript, images used in templates, admin interface assets, or any files you include with your app for use by clients.

Media files are user-generated content—files that are uploaded via your API. These include things like:

Profile pictures uploaded by users

PDFs or documents submitted with forms

Attachments related to tasks, blog posts, or projects

You treat them differently because:

Static files are deployed once and served identically to all users.

Media files are created and accessed at runtime, and may be user-specific.

Both need to be managed correctly in production, especially when you're running Django behind a WSGI server like Gunicorn, which **should not** be responsible for serving files.

Configuring Static Files for Production

First, make sure your settings include the correct paths:

```python
# settings/production.py

STATIC_URL = '/static/'
STATIC_ROOT = BASE_DIR / 'staticfiles'
```

This tells Django where to collect all static files when you're preparing the app for deployment.

Then, collect the files using the management command:

```
python manage.py collectstatic
```

This command scans all installed apps, finds static files, and copies them into the `STATIC_ROOT` directory. This includes things like admin interface stylesheets, DRF's browsable API assets, and anything you've added to `static/` folders in your apps.

Once collected, you don't serve these with Django. Instead, you tell Nginx (or another web server) to serve them directly:

```
location /static/ {
    alias /path/to/your/project/staticfiles/;
}
```

This avoids wasting Django's resources on serving static files, and takes advantage of Nginx's speed and caching features.

Handling Media and File Uploads

Media files are different—they're created dynamically when users upload files through your API.

In your production settings, add:

```
MEDIA_URL = '/media/'
MEDIA_ROOT = BASE_DIR / 'media'
```

This is where Django will write any uploaded files. You then need to configure your API to handle file uploads correctly in your serializers and views.

Suppose users can upload a profile image. You'd start by updating your model:

```
# users/models.py

from django.contrib.auth.models import AbstractUser
from django.db import models

class User(AbstractUser):
    profile_picture =
models.ImageField(upload_to='profile_pics/',
null=True, blank=True)
```

When a user uploads an image, Django stores it in `MEDIA_ROOT/profile_pics/`.

Here's the serializer:

```
# users/serializers.py

from rest_framework import serializers
```

```
from .models import User

class UserSerializer(serializers.ModelSerializer):
    class Meta:
        model = User
        fields = ['username', 'email',
'profile_picture']
```

In the API, file uploads must be handled as `multipart/form-data` requests. DRF does this automatically when the request comes with the correct content type.

On the frontend, the request might look like:

```
const formData = new FormData()
formData.append('profile_picture', file)
formData.append('username', 'janedoe')

fetch('/api/users/5/', {
  method: 'PATCH',
  headers: {
    'Authorization': 'Token YOUR_TOKEN_HERE',
  },
  body: formData
})
```

On the backend, DRF processes this using its `MultiPartParser`, which is enabled by default.

You must also ensure that your web server is configured to serve the uploaded media. Add this to your Nginx config:

```
location /media/ {
    alias /path/to/your/project/media/;
}
```

Now files like `/media/profile_pics/janedoe.jpg` can be served directly by Nginx, while Django handles the upload logic securely behind the scenes.

Validating and Securing File Uploads

Always validate what users upload. File uploads can become a security risk if you don't check the file type, size, or content.

You can start by validating file size in your serializer:

```python
def validate_profile_picture(self, file):
    if file.size > 2 * 1024 * 1024:
        raise serializers.ValidationError("Max file size is 2MB.")
    return file
```

You can also restrict file types using content type checking:

```python
import imghdr

def validate_profile_picture(self, file):
    file_type = imghdr.what(file)
    if file_type not in ['jpeg', 'png']:
        raise serializers.ValidationError("Unsupported image type.")
    return file
```

This prevents users from uploading scripts disguised as images, or files that could be used for attacks or abuse.

Serving Static and Media Files in Development

During development, Django can serve static and media files directly—but only because you're not running behind a production web server.

To enable this in `urls.py`:

```python
from django.conf import settings

from django.conf.urls.static import static

urlpatterns = [
    ...
]

if settings.DEBUG:
    urlpatterns += static(settings.MEDIA_URL, document_root=settings.MEDIA_ROOT)
    urlpatterns += static(settings.STATIC_URL, document_root=settings.STATIC_ROOT)
```

This lets you test file uploads and static rendering without needing Nginx, but it must **never be used in production**.

When your API enters production, file handling becomes a matter of responsibility. Django takes care of storing and processing uploads. Your web server should take care of serving those files efficiently. And your code should take responsibility for validating, restricting, and securing what users upload.

Here's what you've implemented:

Collected all static files into a single deployable directory

Configured Django to store uploads in a designated media directory

Set up your API to accept and process file uploads using `multipart/form-data`

Validated file content and size to avoid abuse

Configured Nginx to serve both `/static/` and `/media/` files without burdening Django

Now your API is equipped to handle real-world usage, from displaying user avatars to serving stylesheets in the admin—all without compromising speed, safety, or maintainability.

Logging, Error Handling, and Monitoring

When your API is running in production, you no longer have the luxury of error tracebacks in the console or real-time debugging tools at your fingertips. Instead, you need a structured way to know what's happening inside your application—especially when something goes wrong. That's where logging, error handling, and monitoring come in.

A reliable Django REST API doesn't just respond to requests. It provides visibility. It logs every important event, surfaces unexpected failures, and gives you the ability to diagnose issues without asking users to "reproduce the bug." In this section, you'll configure Django's built-in logging, set up custom error handling, and wire in an external monitoring service like Sentry for production-grade observability.

Why Logging Is Non-Negotiable in Production

In development, print statements might be enough to trace what's going on. But in production, you need structured logs. Logs help you answer questions like:

Did the request make it to the view?

What was the payload?

Was the request successful or did it raise an exception?

How long did it take?

What SQL queries were executed?

Logging also plays a central role in security, auditing, debugging, and system health checks. Without it, you're operating blindly.

Basic Logging Setup in Django

Django provides a flexible logging system based on Python's `logging` module. You can configure loggers, handlers, formatters, and levels.

Here's a basic production-ready logging setup in your `settings/production.py`:

```
LOGGING = {
    'version': 1,
    'disable_existing_loggers': False,

    'formatters': {
        'verbose': {
            'format': '[{levelname}] {asctime}
{name} - {message}',
            'style': '{',
        },
    },

    'handlers': {
        'file': {
            'level': 'WARNING',
            'class': 'logging.FileHandler',
```

```python
            'filename': BASE_DIR /
'logs/django.log',
            'formatter': 'verbose',
        },
        'console': {
            'level': 'INFO',
            'class': 'logging.StreamHandler',
            'formatter': 'verbose',
        },
    },

    'loggers': {
        'django': {
            'handlers': ['file', 'console'],
            'level': 'INFO',
            'propagate': True,
        },
        'django.request': {
            'handlers': ['file'],
            'level': 'WARNING',
            'propagate': False,
        },
        'your_app': {
            'handlers': ['file'],
            'level': 'INFO',
            'propagate': True,
        }
    }
}
```

This configuration:

Sends warnings and errors to a file (`logs/django.log`)

Outputs info-level logs to the console (for container logs or `systemctl` journal)

Applies different levels to different loggers (you might want more detail from your own app)

Using Logs in Your Code

Once logging is configured, you can start writing logs in your views, services, or anywhere else in your codebase.

```python
# tasks/views.py

import logging
logger = logging.getLogger(__name__)

class TaskViewSet(viewsets.ModelViewSet):
    ...

    def perform_create(self, serializer):
        task = serializer.save()
        logger.info(f"Task created: {task.title} by
{self.request.user.username}")
```

Log responsibly. Avoid logging sensitive data like passwords or tokens. But do log enough to reconstruct what went wrong if a request fails.

Logging SQL Queries (Optional)

To troubleshoot performance issues or confirm that `select_related()` and `prefetch_related()` are working, you can temporarily enable SQL query logging:

```python
LOGGING['loggers']['django.db.backends'] = {
    'handlers': ['console'],
    'level': 'DEBUG',
}
```

This should not be used in production permanently, but it's a helpful tool when you need to audit how the ORM is performing under real load.

Custom Error Responses in Django REST Framework

By default, DRF returns helpful error responses, but they may not match what your frontend needs—or you may want to suppress internal details in production.

You can customize DRF's exception handler like this:

```python
# core/exceptions.py
```

```python
from rest_framework.views import exception_handler

def custom_exception_handler(exc, context):
    response = exception_handler(exc, context)

    if response is not None:
        response.data['status_code'] =
response.status_code

    return response
```

Then configure it in `settings.py`:

```python
REST_FRAMEWORK = {
    'EXCEPTION_HANDLER':
'core.exceptions.custom_exception_handler',
}
```

This gives you full control over what the API returns during errors. You could also log errors here centrally:

```python
import logging
logger = logging.getLogger(__name__)

def custom_exception_handler(exc, context):
    response = exception_handler(exc, context)

    if response is None:
        logger.error(f"Unhandled error: {exc}",
exc_info=True)
    else:
        logger.warning(f"Handled error:
{response.data}")

    return response
```

Now every unhandled exception will appear in your logs with a traceback.

Monitoring and Alerting with Sentry

Sentry is one of the most popular tools for monitoring Django APIs in production. It captures errors, logs context like request data and user information, and lets you see what went wrong without needing direct access to the server.

Install Sentry:

```
pip install --upgrade sentry-sdk
```

Then initialize it in your `production.py`:

```
import sentry_sdk
from sentry_sdk.integrations.django import
DjangoIntegration

sentry_sdk.init(
    dsn=env('SENTRY_DSN'),
    integrations=[DjangoIntegration()],
    traces_sample_rate=0.5,  # Adjust for
performance profiling
    send_default_pii=True,   # Include user info if
available
)
```

Set the SENTRY_DSN environment variable using the DSN provided in your Sentry project settings.

Now, whenever an exception occurs, you'll see:

A complete traceback

The view or method where the error originated

The request path, method, headers, and payload

The user who made the request (if authenticated)

The server environment (host, environment variables, etc.)

You can even configure alerting to email you or send Slack messages when critical issues are detected.

Health Checks and Endpoint Monitoring

For production uptime and basic health validation, it's good practice to expose a simple health-check endpoint:

```
# core/views.py

from rest_framework.response import Response
from rest_framework.views import APIView

class HealthCheckView(APIView):
    authentication_classes = []
    permission_classes = []

    def get(self, request):
        return Response({'status': 'ok'})
```

Add this to your URLs:

```
path('health/', HealthCheckView.as_view()),
```

This endpoint can be monitored by your load balancer, uptime service, or monitoring agent to confirm the app is still responding.

Logging and monitoring aren't optional in production—they're the tools that keep your API observable, debuggable, and maintainable under real-world usage. When things break, you need to know where, why, and how to fix them—before your users even report a problem.

Dockerizing Your Django API

When you're preparing your Django REST API for production, one of the most important steps is packaging your application in a reliable, portable, and reproducible way. That's exactly what Docker helps you achieve.

By containerizing your Django app with Docker, you're building a standardized unit that contains your application code, dependencies, system packages, environment configuration, and runtime behavior—all bundled into a single image that can run consistently across development, staging, and production environments.

Every developer's local environment is slightly different—different Python versions, installed packages, OS-level dependencies, and ways of installing PostgreSQL or Redis. Docker eliminates this inconsistency by running your app in a container with everything pre-defined.

In production, containers give you:

Portability across cloud providers and servers

Consistent builds between developers and CI pipelines

Easy scaling with orchestration (like Kubernetes or Docker Swarm)

Simpler rollback and version pinning with immutable images

Let's start by building the actual container image for your API.

Writing a Production-Grade Dockerfile

Here's a clean, practical `Dockerfile` for your Django API:

```
# Dockerfile

FROM python:3.11-slim

ENV PYTHONDONTWRITEBYTECODE 1
ENV PYTHONUNBUFFERED 1

WORKDIR /code

RUN apt-get update && apt-get install -y \
    build-essential \
    libpq-dev \
    --no-install-recommends && rm -rf
/var/lib/apt/lists/*

COPY requirements.txt /code/
RUN pip install --upgrade pip && pip install --no-
cache-dir -r requirements.txt

COPY . /code/

CMD ["gunicorn", "your_project.wsgi:application",
"--bind", "0.0.0.0:8000"]
```

What's happening here:

You're starting with a minimal Python 3.11 base image (`slim` variant).

You disable bytecode and force Python to flush stdout immediately.

System packages like `libpq-dev` are installed to compile PostgreSQL bindings.

You install all Python dependencies from `requirements.txt`.

The final command runs your Django app using Gunicorn—ready for production.

You can now build the image:

```
docker build -t django-api .
```

Then run it:

```
docker run -p 8000:8000 django-api
```

If you've set up your Django app to use environment variables correctly (as described in earlier chapters), the container will work as expected as long as you pass the necessary variables.

Using docker-compose for Multi-Container Setup

In production, you're usually running Django alongside other services like PostgreSQL, Redis, or Celery. `docker-compose` allows you to define all services in a single YAML file.

Here's a `docker-compose.yml` file that includes Django and PostgreSQL:

```
version: '3.9'

services:
  db:
    image: postgres:15
    environment:
      POSTGRES_DB: mydb
      POSTGRES_USER: myuser
      POSTGRES_PASSWORD: mypassword
    volumes:
      - postgres_data:/var/lib/postgresql/data
    restart: always

  web:
    build: .
```

```
      command: gunicorn your_project.wsgi:application
--bind 0.0.0.0:8000
    volumes:
      - .:/code
    ports:
      - "8000:8000"
    depends_on:
      - db
    environment:
      DJANGO_SECRET_KEY: your-secret-key
      DJANGO_DEBUG: "False"
      DATABASE_URL:
postgres://myuser:mypassword@db:5432/mydb
    restart: always

volumes:
  postgres_data:
```

This setup does the following:

Spins up a PostgreSQL container with preconfigured credentials

Builds and runs your Django app using the Dockerfile

Injects environment variables into the container

Uses Docker networking to connect Django to PostgreSQL using the hostname db

You can bring everything up with one command:

```
docker-compose up --build
```

This starts both services and connects them together in a shared network.

Handling Static Files and Media in Docker

In production, your static files and media must be collected and served outside of Django (usually with Nginx).

You can add volume mounts in Docker to persist these files:

```
    volumes:
      - ./staticfiles:/code/staticfiles
      - ./media:/code/media
```

Then make sure your `settings.py` contains:

```
STATIC_ROOT = BASE_DIR / 'staticfiles'
MEDIA_ROOT = BASE_DIR / 'media'
```

To collect static files inside the container:

```
docker-compose exec web python manage.py
collectstatic --noinput
```

The `staticfiles/` directory will now contain all your assets, ready to be served by a reverse proxy or CDN.

Managing Environment Variables Securely

Avoid hardcoding secrets in your `docker-compose.yml`. Instead, use an `.env` file:

```
DJANGO_SECRET_KEY=super-secret-key
DJANGO_DEBUG=False
DATABASE_URL=postgres://myuser:mypassword@db:5432/m
ydb
```

Then reference it in `docker-compose.yml`:

```
env_file:
  - .env
```

This keeps your secrets out of source control and lets you maintain separate config for local development and production deployment.

Running Django Management Commands

Sometimes you need to run Django commands like `migrate` or `createsuperuser` inside your container.

You can run:

```
docker-compose exec web python manage.py migrate
```
Or create a user:

```
docker-compose exec web python manage.py
createsuperuser
```

These commands run inside the Django container with access to the same environment configuration.

Health Checks and Container Restarts

To make your Dockerized API more production-ready, you should also add health checks and automatic restarts:

```
web:
    ...
    restart: always
    healthcheck:
        test: ["CMD-SHELL", "curl -f
http://localhost:8000/health/ || exit 1"]
        interval: 30s
        timeout: 10s
        retries: 5
```

This ensures that if the Django app crashes or becomes unresponsive, Docker will restart it automatically and report its health status.

Docker gives you a way to run your Django API consistently—locally, in staging, or in production—with full control over its runtime environment and dependencies.

Once you've containerized your Django API, deployment becomes a repeatable and predictable task. It no longer matters whether you're running this on AWS, DigitalOcean, Azure, or a bare-metal server—you have full control of how your app runs. In the next section, you'll complete this picture by deploying it behind Nginx and PostgreSQL, ready to serve real users.

Deployment with Gunicorn, Nginx, and PostgreSQL

Once your Django REST API is ready, fully tested, and containerized, the final step is deploying it to a production server where it can reliably serve real users. In production, your application needs to be available 24/7, respond efficiently to concurrent requests, serve static and media files, and stay connected to a robust database backend.

The most common and proven deployment stack for Django includes **Gunicorn** as the application server, **Nginx** as the reverse proxy and static file handler, and **PostgreSQL** as the production-grade relational database. This setup separates responsibilities cleanly and allows your application to scale while remaining performant and secure.

How the Components Work Together

Understanding how Gunicorn, Nginx, and PostgreSQL interact helps you troubleshoot and scale later.

Gunicorn runs your Django application as a WSGI server. It handles Python code execution and application logic.

Nginx receives incoming HTTP requests. It serves static files directly, passes API requests to Gunicorn, and can terminate SSL/TLS.

PostgreSQL stores your application data. Django interacts with it using `psycopg2` or another PostgreSQL driver.

The flow looks like this:

```
Client Browser ——> Nginx ——> Gunicorn ——> Django
——> PostgreSQL
```

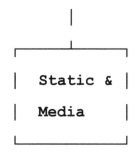

```
                    |
          ┌─────────┴─────────┐
          |    Static &  |
          |    Media     |
          └───────────────────┘
```

Let's break down how to deploy this setup on a Linux server.

Step 1: Set Up Your Server

Provision a virtual machine (such as on DigitalOcean, AWS EC2, or a bare-metal server). Ensure it runs a modern Linux distribution (Ubuntu 22.04 is a safe default).

Update the system:

```
sudo apt update && sudo apt upgrade -y
```

Install required system packages:

```
sudo apt install python3-pip python3-venv
postgresql postgresql-contrib nginx curl git -y
```

Create a dedicated system user for your app:

```
sudo adduser djangoapi --disabled-password
```

Switch to this user:

```
sudo su - djangoapi
```

Step 2: Configure PostgreSQL for Production

Log into the PostgreSQL shell:

```
sudo -u postgres psql
```

Create a production database and user:

```
CREATE DATABASE apidb;
CREATE USER apidbuser WITH PASSWORD
'securepassword';
ALTER ROLE apidbuser SET client_encoding TO 'utf8';
ALTER ROLE apidbuser SET
default_transaction_isolation TO 'read committed';
ALTER ROLE apidbuser SET timezone TO 'UTC';
GRANT ALL PRIVILEGES ON DATABASE apidb TO
apidbuser;
\q
```

Update your Django `settings.py` to use this database:

```
DATABASES = {
    'default': {
        'ENGINE': 'django.db.backends.postgresql',
        'NAME': 'apidb',
        'USER': 'apidbuser',
        'PASSWORD': 'securepassword',
        'HOST': 'localhost',
        'PORT': '5432',
    }
```

```
}
```

Step 3: Install Your Application

Clone your project into the home directory:

```
git clone https://github.com/your-org/your-api-
project.git
cd your-api-project
```

Create a virtual environment:

```
python3 -m venv venv
source venv/bin/activate
```

Install dependencies:

```
pip install --upgrade pip
pip install -r requirements.txt
```

Set up your `.env` or production `settings.py` file with the correct database credentials, `DEBUG=False`, and a strong secret key.

Run migrations and collect static files:

```
python manage.py migrate
python manage.py collectstatic --noinput
```

Create a superuser if needed:

```
python manage.py createsuperuser
```

Step 4: Run Django with Gunicorn

Install Gunicorn in your virtual environment:

```
pip install gunicorn
```

Run Gunicorn manually to verify:

```
gunicorn your_project.wsgi:application --bind
127.0.0.1:8000
```

If this works, set up a systemd service to manage Gunicorn:

```
sudo nano /etc/systemd/system/gunicorn.service
```

Paste the following:

```
[Unit]
Description=Gunicorn daemon for Django API
After=network.target

[Service]
User=djangoapi
Group=www-data
WorkingDirectory=/home/djangoapi/your-api-project
ExecStart=/home/djangoapi/your-api-
project/venv/bin/gunicorn \
        --access-logfile - \
        --workers 3 \
        --bind 127.0.0.1:8000 \
        your_project.wsgi:application

[Install]
WantedBy=multi-user.target
```
Reload systemd and start Gunicorn:
```
sudo systemctl daemon-reexec
sudo systemctl daemon-reload
sudo systemctl start gunicorn
sudo systemctl enable gunicorn
```

Check the status:

```
sudo systemctl status gunicorn
```

Step 5: Configure Nginx as a Reverse Proxy

Create a new Nginx site configuration:

```
sudo nano /etc/nginx/sites-available/djangoapi
```

Paste this:

```
server {
    listen 80;
    server_name yourdomain.com;

    location /static/ {
        alias /home/djangoapi/your-api-
project/staticfiles/;
```

```
    }

    location /media/ {
        alias /home/djangoapi/your-api-
project/media/;
    }

    location / {
        proxy_pass http://127.0.0.1:8000;
        proxy_set_header Host $host;
        proxy_set_header X-Real-IP $remote_addr;
        proxy_set_header X-Forwarded-For
$proxy_add_x_forwarded_for;
        proxy_set_header X-Forwarded-Proto $scheme;
    }
}
```

Enable the site:

```
sudo ln -s /etc/nginx/sites-available/djangoapi
/etc/nginx/sites-enabled/
sudo nginx -t
sudo systemctl restart nginx
```

Now you can access your Django API at `http://yourdomain.com/`.

Step 6: Add HTTPS with Let's Encrypt

Secure your API using a free TLS certificate:

```
sudo apt install certbot python3-certbot-nginx -y
sudo certbot --nginx -d yourdomain.com
```

Let's Encrypt will automatically install a certificate and configure Nginx to redirect HTTP to HTTPS.

At this point, you've completed a full-stack production deployment of your Django REST API using Gunicorn, Nginx, and PostgreSQL. Here's what's in place:

Gunicorn is running your Django app as a high-performance WSGI server

Nginx is handling incoming HTTP requests, SSL termination, and static files

PostgreSQL is managing your relational data securely

Systemd is managing the Gunicorn process, keeping it alive

Your server is protected with HTTPS via Let's Encrypt

This setup is fast, secure, and scalable. You can easily add load balancing, backups, monitoring, and container orchestration later, but this structure gives you a solid foundation for real production usage.

From here, your API is no longer just code—it's a deployed, fully operational service.

Chapter 10: Documentation, CI/CD, and Beyond

By now, you've built a production-grade Django REST API: feature-complete, secure, tested, and deployed. But building the API is only part of your responsibility. You also need to document it clearly, automate its deployment reliably, keep it performant under load, and prepare for future architectural growth.

This chapter is all about what comes next. You'll start by exposing your API documentation with Swagger and ReDoc, explore best practices for versioning and maintaining backward compatibility, build a CI/CD pipeline with GitHub Actions, and explore practical strategies for scaling and performance tuning. Finally, we'll talk about what lies ahead: async views, background tasks with Celery, and the early stages of transitioning to microservices when needed.

Auto-Generating API Docs with Swagger and ReDoc

When you build an API, writing the code is only half the responsibility. The other half is communicating how that API works. This becomes especially important when your API is used by a frontend team, external developers, or third-party integrators. Even if the backend is solid, without clear documentation, you'll end up answering repetitive questions—or worse, users will give up trying to use the API at all.

You can write API docs manually, but in practice, that becomes tedious and error-prone. What you really want is for your API documentation to generate itself, directly from your views, serializers, and models. This is where tools like **Swagger** and **ReDoc**—powered by the **OpenAPI specification**—come into play.

Django REST Framework doesn't ship with built-in OpenAPI generation, but it has first-class support through libraries like `drf-spectacular`. This gives you full OpenAPI schema generation and beautiful interactive UIs, all without duplicating your documentation effort.

Installing and Configuring drf-spectacular

The most reliable and feature-complete tool for OpenAPI documentation in DRF is `drf-spectacular`.

Start by installing it:

```
pip install drf-spectacular
```

Then register it in your Django settings:

```python
# settings.py

INSTALLED_APPS += [
    'drf_spectacular',
]

REST_FRAMEWORK = {
    'DEFAULT_SCHEMA_CLASS':
'drf_spectacular.openapi.AutoSchema',
}
```

You can now expose your schema as a URL and add Swagger or ReDoc UI endpoints.

In your root `urls.py`:

```python
from drf_spectacular.views import
SpectacularAPIView, SpectacularSwaggerView,
SpectacularRedocView

urlpatterns = [
    path('api/schema/',
SpectacularAPIView.as_view(), name='schema'),
    path('api/docs/',
SpectacularSwaggerView.as_view(url_name='schema'),
name='swagger-ui'),
    path('api/redoc/',
SpectacularRedocView.as_view(url_name='schema'),
name='redoc'),
]
```

After starting your server, you can visit:

`/api/docs/` to interact with your API using Swagger UI

`/api/redoc/` for a clean, structured ReDoc interface

`/api/schema/` to get the raw OpenAPI JSON schema

What You Get Out of the Box

The beauty of `drf-spectacular` is that it works immediately with your existing views and serializers.

If you've defined a typical DRF view like this:

```
from rest_framework import viewsets
from .models import Task
from .serializers import TaskSerializer

class TaskViewSet(viewsets.ModelViewSet):
    queryset = Task.objects.all()
    serializer_class = TaskSerializer
```

The generated documentation will include:

The list of endpoints (`/api/tasks/`, `/api/tasks/{id}/`)

Allowed methods per endpoint (GET, POST, PUT, DELETE)

Parameters such as `id`, `status`, or query filters

Field-level documentation including types, choices, and requirements

There's no extra effort required. Your API becomes self-documenting simply by following DRF conventions.

Customizing Your API Schema

While the automatic generation is great, there are times when you want more control—maybe you need to describe an undocumented parameter, change the field description, or adjust tags and summaries for clarity.

To override or extend the schema, you can use `@extend_schema` decorators:

```
from drf_spectacular.utils import extend_schema
from rest_framework.decorators import api_view
from rest_framework.response import Response
```

```
@extend_schema(
    summary="Returns the current API version",
    description="This endpoint returns metadata
about the API version and build time.",
    responses={200: dict},
)
@api_view(['GET'])
def version_info(request):
    return Response({
        "version": "v1.0.0",
        "build": "2024-04-01T10:00:00Z"
    })
```

You can also annotate serializers:

```
from drf_spectacular.utils import OpenApiExample,
extend_schema_serializer

@extend_schema_serializer(
    examples=[
        OpenApiExample(
            'Valid Input',
            value={'title': 'Test Task', 'status':
'todo'}
        )
    ]
)
class TaskSerializer(serializers.ModelSerializer):
    ...
```

These customizations improve clarity for consumers of your API, without affecting behavior or adding redundancy.

Documenting Auth and Permissions

One of the most misunderstood aspects of an API—especially for frontend developers—is how to authenticate.

You can configure how authentication is documented using SPECTACULAR_SETTINGS in settings.py:

```
SPECTACULAR_SETTINGS = {
```

```
    'TITLE': 'Task Manager API',
    'DESCRIPTION': 'A backend API for managing
projects and tasks',
    'VERSION': '1.0.0',
    'SERVE_INCLUDE_SCHEMA': False,
    'SWAGGER_UI_SETTINGS': {
        'persistAuthorization': True,
    },
    'COMPONENT_SPLIT_REQUEST': True,
    'SECURITY': [{'TokenAuth': []}],
    'SECURITY_SCHEMES': {
        'TokenAuth': {
            'type': 'http',
            'scheme': 'bearer',
            'bearerFormat': 'Token',
        }
    },
}
```

Now users can enter their auth token directly in the Swagger UI and test endpoints as if they were logged in. That dramatically improves developer onboarding and reduces mistakes during frontend/backend integration.

Using ReDoc for Public API Portals

While Swagger is great for internal teams, many developers prefer **ReDoc** for public API documentation. It's clean, responsive, and feels like a static knowledge base.

If you're building a public API for third-party clients, `/api/redoc/` becomes a professional-looking documentation portal. You can customize titles, add branding, and even self-host it using the exported OpenAPI JSON from `/api/schema/`.

Exporting the Schema for External Use

To generate the raw schema as a file:

```
python manage.py spectacular --file schema.yaml
```

This is helpful for:

Uploading to an API gateway (e.g., Kong, AWS API Gateway)

Generating client SDKs using tools like OpenAPI Generator

Integrating with third-party API testers or mock servers

Once exported, you can generate code in dozens of languages:

```
openapi-generator-cli generate \
  -i schema.yaml \
  -g typescript-fetch \
  -o frontend-sdk/
```

That saves your frontend team hours of manual work and prevents inconsistencies between backend and frontend contracts.

By integrating automatic OpenAPI documentation using `drf-spectacular`, you've turned your API into a developer-friendly product. It explains itself, defines expectations clearly, and supports interactive exploration—without writing a separate doc site.

And most importantly, you've set the standard for professional API delivery. Good documentation isn't a feature—it's a responsibility. And now your API fulfills it automatically.

API Versioning and Change Management

As you continue developing and refining your Django REST API, change is inevitable. You'll need to introduce new features, update behaviors, or remove deprecated fields and endpoints. And when your API is consumed by frontend applications or external clients, those changes can break things—sometimes silently.

Versioning is your solution to this problem. By supporting multiple versions of your API, you can release new behavior without breaking existing integrations. This gives you the flexibility to evolve your API while giving your users the time and space to adapt.

When you expose an API to external systems, you're making a contract: "Here's how this endpoint behaves, and here's what it returns."

If a client application calls `/api/tasks/` and expects a field like `status`, and you later remove or rename that field, you've broken the contract. If a frontend developer expects the response to include pagination in a certain format, and you switch to a different scheme, you've broken it again.

These types of changes—removing fields, changing data formats, modifying authentication or validation rules—are often necessary. But they should never surprise users.

Versioning gives you a way to make changes **without disrupting current users**. You keep old versions functional while offering new versions with improved logic, updated formats, or breaking changes.

Enabling Versioning in Django REST Framework

Django REST Framework supports multiple versioning strategies. The most practical and explicit is **URL path versioning**.

Enable it in your settings:

```
# settings.py

REST_FRAMEWORK = {
    ...
    'DEFAULT_VERSIONING_CLASS':
'rest_framework.versioning.URLPathVersioning',
    'DEFAULT_VERSION': 'v1',
    'ALLOWED_VERSIONS': ['v1', 'v2'],
}
```

Now you'll structure your API URLs to include the version:

```
# project/urls.py

from django.urls import path, include

urlpatterns = [
    path('api/v1/', include('api.v1.urls')),
    path('api/v2/', include('api.v2.urls')),
]
```

Each version gets its own dedicated `urls.py` and potentially its own views, serializers, or logic.

For example:

```
api/
├── v1/
│   ├── views.py
│   ├── serializers.py
│   └── urls.py
├── v2/
│   ├── views.py
│   ├── serializers.py
│   └── urls.py
```

This lets you isolate changes. You might rewrite a serializer in v2, or alter a business rule in a viewset—without impacting v1.

Practical Example: Changing Response Format in v2

Suppose you initially returned task data in v1 like this:

```
{
  "id": 5,
  "title": "Finish documentation",
  "status": "todo"
}
```

In v2, you want to include more metadata, like timestamps and a nested project object. You can implement this in a new serializer:

```python
# api/v2/serializers.py

from rest_framework import serializers
from tasks.models import Task

class
TaskV2Serializer(serializers.ModelSerializer):
```

```
    project_name =
serializers.CharField(source='project.name',
read_only=True)

    class Meta:
        model = Task
        fields = ['id', 'title', 'status',
'created_at', 'updated_at', 'project_name']
```

Then update your viewset in v2/views.py:

```
from rest_framework import viewsets
from tasks.models import Task
from .serializers import TaskV2Serializer

class TaskViewSet(viewsets.ModelViewSet):
    queryset = Task.objects.all()
    serializer_class = TaskV2Serializer
```

And wire it up in v2/urls.py:

```
from django.urls import path, include
from rest_framework.routers import DefaultRouter
from .views import TaskViewSet

router = DefaultRouter()
router.register('tasks', TaskViewSet,
basename='task')

urlpatterns = router.urls
```

Now users of v1 see the old format. Users of v2 get the new fields. And both are correct.

Communicating Breaking Changes

Versioning helps you ship breaking changes safely, but it doesn't eliminate your responsibility to communicate them. You should document:

Which versions exist and what changed between them

When support for older versions will be dropped (if ever)

Which version is considered stable or recommended

This information belongs in your OpenAPI schema and developer docs. You can include version descriptions with `drf-spectacular` using `SPECTACULAR_SETTINGS`:

```
SPECTACULAR_SETTINGS = {
    'VERSION': 'v2',
    'TITLE': 'Task API',
    'DESCRIPTION': 'Current stable version of the
Task API. Older versions available at /api/v1/',
}
```

You can also make older versions **read-only** once they're deprecated:

```
class
DeprecatedTaskViewSet(viewsets.ReadOnlyModelViewSet
):
    ...
```

This prevents new writes while keeping data accessible.

Supporting Multiple Versions in One Codebase

It's entirely possible to support `v1` and `v2` without duplicating your entire codebase. Here's how:

Reuse models and shared logic between versions

Only split serializers and views where behavior has changed

Use base viewsets or serializers to keep shared functionality DRY

For example:

```
# shared.py

class
BaseTaskSerializer(serializers.ModelSerializer):
    class Meta:
        model = Task
        fields = ['id', 'title', 'status']
```

Then extend it in `v2`:

```
class TaskV2Serializer(BaseTaskSerializer):
```

```
    project_name =
serializers.CharField(source='project.name',
read_only=True)

    class Meta(BaseTaskSerializer.Meta):
        fields = BaseTaskSerializer.Meta.fields +
['project_name']
```

This keeps your code maintainable as your API evolves.

Strategies for Sunsetting Old Versions

Eventually, you'll want to retire outdated versions. Don't just delete them. Plan for a smooth transition:

Announce deprecation early. Provide at least 6–12 months' notice.

Communicate via HTTP headers. Add a deprecation warning:

```
def finalize_response(self, request, response,
*args, **kwargs):
    if request.version == 'v1':
        response['X-API-Warning'] = 'v1 will be
removed on 2025-01-01'
    return super().finalize_response(request,
response, *args, **kwargs)
```

Offer migration guides. Explain how to switch from v1 to v2.

Log traffic by version. Monitor usage of old versions before removing them.

Only remove versions when traffic is low and migration support is well documented.

Versioning isn't just a technical feature. It's part of your API's lifecycle management. Without it, you risk breaking downstream systems, forcing unwanted upgrades, and frustrating developers who depend on your API.

You've now implemented:

Explicit versioning through URL paths

Isolated code structures for v1, v2, and beyond

Controlled rollout of new features and response formats

Practices for deprecating and sunsetting old versions safely

With versioning in place, your API is no longer rigid. It's an evolving product—capable of adapting to new requirements without sacrificing stability for existing users.

Creating a CI/CD Pipeline with GitHub Actions

Once your Django REST API is written, tested, and deployed, it's time to automate the process. That's what Continuous Integration and Continuous Deployment (CI/CD) is all about—replacing manual steps with automated workflows that handle testing, building, and deployment every time you push code.

By adopting a CI/CD pipeline early, you reduce risk, prevent regressions, and deploy updates faster. You'll catch problems sooner—before they reach production—and eliminate the need for developers to run long, manual release steps. It turns every pull request and commit into a verified unit of work.

With a well-configured pipeline, GitHub Actions can:

Run tests for every commit and pull request

Set up a PostgreSQL database to test your Django code against

Block a merge if any test fails

Optionally deploy your Dockerized app when changes hit your `main` or `release` branch

This means you'll know, without question, that a branch is ready to ship—because it has passed the same process that all working code goes through.

Let's start by setting up the most essential part: testing your Django API automatically.

Step 1: Create Your Workflow File

In your Django project root, create a folder named `.github/workflows`. Inside that folder, create a file named `ci.yml`.

```
mkdir -p .github/workflows
touch .github/workflows/ci.yml
```

Now open `ci.yml` and define your pipeline:

```yaml
name: Django API CI

on:
  push:
    branches: [main]
  pull_request:
    branches: [main]

jobs:
  test:
    runs-on: ubuntu-latest

    services:
      postgres:
        image: postgres:15
        env:
          POSTGRES_DB: testdb
          POSTGRES_USER: testuser
          POSTGRES_PASSWORD: testpass
        ports:
          - 5432:5432
        options: >-
          --health-cmd pg_isready
          --health-interval 10s
          --health-timeout 5s
          --health-retries 5

    env:
      DATABASE_URL:
postgres://testuser:testpass@localhost:5432/testdb
      DJANGO_SECRET_KEY: fake
      DJANGO_DEBUG: "False"

    steps:
      - uses: actions/checkout@v3

      - name: Set up Python
        uses: actions/setup-python@v4
```

```
      with:
        python-version: '3.11'

    - name: Install dependencies
      run: |
        python -m pip install --upgrade pip
        pip install -r requirements.txt

    - name: Run Django migrations
      run: |
        python manage.py migrate

    - name: Run tests
      run: |
        pytest --disable-warnings
```

Let's walk through what this does:

It runs whenever you push to `main` or open a pull request against `main`.

It uses a fresh Ubuntu environment with Python 3.11.

It spins up a temporary PostgreSQL service with your test credentials.

It installs all dependencies, runs migrations, and executes your test suite using `pytest`.

This is your **CI pipeline**. Every time you push, GitHub Actions will test your code from scratch using a real database—just like production.

Step 2: Set Up Your Django Project to Use DATABASE_URL

To keep your pipeline configuration clean, update `settings.py` to support a single environment variable for your database connection:

```
# settings.py

import dj_database_url

DATABASES = {
    'default': dj_database_url.config(

default='postgres://user:pass@localhost:5432/dbname
',
```

```
        conn_max_age=600
    )
}
```

Install the dependency:

```
pip install dj-database-url
```

Now your app can connect to any PostgreSQL database using a single DATABASE_URL string, which is easy to override in production or CI.

Step 3: Securing Secrets (Optional)

If you want to test production-like features (email services, third-party APIs, secret keys), you can store secrets in GitHub Actions:

Go to your repository on GitHub

Click **Settings → Secrets → Actions**

Add secrets like DJANGO_SECRET_KEY, SENDGRID_API_KEY, or SENTRY_DSN

In your workflow file:

```
env:
  DJANGO_SECRET_KEY: ${{ secrets.DJANGO_SECRET_KEY }}
```

This keeps secrets out of source control while still making them available in CI.

Step 4: Enforcing CI on All Pull Requests

Once your pipeline is in place, enable **required status checks** in GitHub:

Go to your repository → **Settings → Branches**

Edit the branch protection rules for main

Require status checks to pass before merging

This prevents broken tests from being merged—and ensures only stable, verified code enters your production branch.

Step 5: Adding Optional Deployment Jobs

If you're using Docker and have a container registry or hosting service like Heroku, Fly.io, or AWS ECS, you can add a second job that runs only after tests pass:

```
deploy:
  needs: test
  runs-on: ubuntu-latest
  if: github.ref == 'refs/heads/main'
  steps:
    - uses: actions/checkout@v3
    - name: Log in to Docker
      run: echo "${{ secrets.DOCKER_PASSWORD }}" |
docker login -u "${{ secrets.DOCKER_USERNAME }}" --
password-stdin
    - name: Build and Push Image
      run: |
        docker build -t youruser/api:latest .
        docker push youruser/api:latest
```

This lets you trigger production deployments automatically, with full traceability. Your `main` branch becomes a deployable artifact.

You can also use third-party deployment actions (like for Heroku or Render) if you're not using Docker.

CI/CD isn't just for big teams or enterprise applications. Even a solo developer benefits from having a clean, automated way to verify and deploy their work. With GitHub Actions, you've added professional-grade automation to your Django API without needing an external CI tool or complicated setup.

This kind of automation doesn't just save time—it raises the quality bar for every future update. Your API is now safer, faster to release, and easier to maintain, no matter how big your team or project grows.

Scaling, Caching, and Performance Tuning

Building an API that works well in development is one thing. Building an API that remains fast, responsive, and efficient under real-world traffic and data load is another. Once your Django REST API begins to handle more users, more data, and more requests per second, small performance issues turn into bottlenecks. Poorly indexed queries slow down responses. Redundant database hits add unnecessary load. And repeated calculations waste CPU time.

The first step in tuning is understanding where the time goes. An API request typically breaks down into several parts:

Network overhead: Time for the request to reach the server

View execution: Logic in your Django view or viewset

ORM queries: Time to fetch and serialize data

Serialization: Converting your model instances into JSON

Response delivery: Returning the response over HTTP

Most of the performance gains come from reducing the time spent on ORM queries and unnecessary view logic. That's where we'll focus.

Optimizing ORM Queries with `select_related()` and `prefetch_related()`

One of the most common causes of slow APIs is the **N+1 query problem**. This happens when your code fetches a list of objects and then queries the database once per related object—causing dozens or hundreds of extra queries.

Suppose you have a `Task` model that is related to a `Project`:

```
class Task(models.Model):
    title = models.CharField(max_length=255)
    project = models.ForeignKey(Project,
on_delete=models.CASCADE)
```

In your view:

```
class TaskViewSet(viewsets.ModelViewSet):
    queryset = Task.objects.all()
    serializer_class = TaskSerializer
```

And your serializer accesses `task.project.name`:

```
class TaskSerializer(serializers.ModelSerializer):
```

```
    project_name =
serializers.CharField(source='project.name',
read_only=True)

    class Meta:
        model = Task
        fields = ['id', 'title', 'project_name']
```

This will trigger **one query per task** to fetch the related project. If you're returning 50 tasks, you now have 51 queries. That's inefficient.

Fix it with `select_related()`:

```
class TaskViewSet(viewsets.ModelViewSet):
    def get_queryset(self):
        return
Task.objects.select_related('project')
```

This tells Django to fetch the `project` along with each task in a **single join query**. You can verify the number of queries using Django Debug Toolbar during development.

Use `prefetch_related()` when dealing with `ManyToManyField` or reverse `ForeignKey` relationships:

```
Task.objects.prefetch_related('tags', 'comments')
```

This executes two queries and joins them in Python—faster than executing one query per related object.

Indexing Your Database for High-Volume Filtering

When your API uses `.filter()` heavily on large tables, indexes are essential.

Suppose users can filter tasks by `status`, `priority`, and `assignee_id`. These should be indexed in your model:

```
class Task(models.Model):
    status = models.CharField(max_length=50,
db_index=True)
    priority = models.IntegerField(db_index=True)
```

```
    assignee = models.ForeignKey(User,
on_delete=models.SET_NULL, null=True,
db_index=True)
```

You can also add composite indexes:

```
class Meta:
    indexes = [
        models.Index(fields=['status',
'priority']),
    ]
```

This helps queries like:

```
Task.objects.filter(status='todo', priority=2)
```

Avoid indexing every field. Indexes speed up reads but slow down writes and increase storage usage. Prioritize fields that appear frequently in filters, lookups, and ordering clauses.

Applying Per-View Caching

If an endpoint returns the same response for all users—or changes infrequently—cache it.

Start by installing and configuring a cache backend. For production, Redis is ideal.

```
sudo apt install redis
pip install django-redis
```

In `settings.py`:

```
CACHES = {
    'default': {
        'BACKEND': 'django_redis.cache.RedisCache',
        'LOCATION': 'redis://127.0.0.1:6379/1',
        'OPTIONS': {
            'CLIENT_CLASS':
'django_redis.client.DefaultClient',
        }
    }
}
```

Now apply caching at the view level:

```python
from django.views.decorators.cache import
cache_page
from django.utils.decorators import
method_decorator

@method_decorator(cache_page(60 * 10), name='list')
class TaskViewSet(viewsets.ModelViewSet):
    queryset = Task.objects.all()
    serializer_class = TaskSerializer
```

This caches the `list()` endpoint for 10 minutes. It doesn't hit the database again during that time unless the cache is invalidated.

You can also apply manual caching for custom queries:

```python
from django.core.cache import cache

def get_high_priority_tasks():
    tasks = cache.get('high_priority_tasks')
    if not tasks:
        tasks = Task.objects.filter(priority=5)
        cache.set('high_priority_tasks', tasks,
timeout=300)
    return tasks
```

This gives you full control over cache keys and lifetimes.

Using Pagination to Reduce Payload Size

Without pagination, your API may return thousands of records in a single request. That's not just slow—it's unnecessary and wasteful.

Make sure pagination is enabled:

```python
REST_FRAMEWORK = {
    'DEFAULT_PAGINATION_CLASS':
'rest_framework.pagination.PageNumberPagination',
    'PAGE_SIZE': 25,
}
```

This keeps your responses small and your endpoints responsive, especially on mobile or slow networks.

You can also use `LimitOffsetPagination` or create custom pagination classes to match frontend requirements.

Asynchronous Tasks for Long-Running Operations

Some operations shouldn't be handled in the main request thread. These include:

Sending emails

Generating reports

Processing uploaded files

Syncing with third-party APIs

Use **Celery** for background tasks:

```
pip install celery redis
```

In `celery.py`:

```
import os
from celery import Celery

os.environ.setdefault('DJANGO_SETTINGS_MODULE',
'your_project.settings')
app = Celery('your_project')
app.config_from_object('django.conf:settings',
namespace='CELERY')
app.autodiscover_tasks()
```

In a task module:

```
from celery import shared_task

@shared_task
def send_welcome_email(user_id):
    ...
```

Now you can call it like:

```
send_welcome_email.delay(user.id)
```

This moves the work into Redis-backed background queues, freeing up your API thread instantly.

Profiling API Performance

Use tools to inspect and monitor your API under real usage:

Django Debug Toolbar (for development): shows query counts, SQL, and timing.

New Relic / Datadog / Sentry Performance: for real-time production profiling.

Gunicorn + Prometheus Exporter: to track latency, memory, and throughput.

Always measure before you optimize. Guessing rarely yields the best results.

Horizontal Scaling and Load Balancing

When a single instance isn't enough, run multiple instances behind a load balancer. Each instance of your Django API should be stateless—able to handle any request, independent of previous requests.

You can use:

Docker containers: deploy your app as repeatable units

NGINX or HAProxy: to distribute traffic between Gunicorn workers

Cloud load balancers (AWS ELB, GCP Load Balancer, etc.)

Use health checks to monitor instance readiness and auto-restart dead processes with systemd or Docker restart policies.

Performance tuning is about removing bottlenecks before they become outages. It's a combination of better queries, smarter data access, and infrastructure awareness.

Next Steps: Async APIs, Celery, and Microservices

Once your Django REST API is mature and serving real users, there comes a point where new demands force you to go further. Some endpoints need to respond faster. Others need to handle long-running tasks without blocking. You may even need to break your API into smaller, specialized services as your team or system grows.

This section introduces you to three advanced directions you'll eventually consider:

Building asynchronous endpoints to improve concurrency

Offloading background work with Celery

Structuring your system using microservices

Each of these solves real problems that appear as your application scales—so rather than treat them like abstract ideas, we'll explore their exact use cases and show how to implement them safely in a Django-based environment.

Using Async Views in Django

As of Django 3.1+, you can write asynchronous views using Python's async def syntax. These are useful when your view needs to wait on I/O like an external API or slow database call—but doesn't do any CPU-heavy work.

Let's say you want to query an external microservice to check a user's subscription status:

```
pip install httpx
```

Now, you can use an async view like this:

```
# subscriptions/views.py

import httpx
from django.http import JsonResponse
from rest_framework.views import APIView

class SubscriptionStatusView(APIView):
    async def get(self, request, user_id):
        async with httpx.AsyncClient() as client:
            response = await
client.get(f"https://subscriptions.internal/api/use
rs/{user_id}/status")
```

```
        data = response.json()
        return JsonResponse({"status":
data.get("status")})
```

This view does not block the main thread while waiting for the external API. Django passes control back to the event loop, freeing up the server to handle other requests during that wait.

This works best with ASGI servers like Uvicorn or Daphne. If you're running Gunicorn, switch to using the uvicorn worker:

```
gunicorn your_project.asgi:application -k
uvicorn.workers.UvicornWorker
```

Use async views only where needed. If a view just hits the database and does local logic, async won't help and may add complexity.

Background Tasks with Celery

Even with async views, some tasks just don't belong in the request/response cycle. These include:

Sending emails

Processing uploaded media

Generating reports

Sending webhooks

Performing third-party sync jobs

For anything that might take more than a second or two—or might fail independently—you want to use a background job queue. Celery is the gold standard in Python for this.

Start by installing:

```
pip install celery redis
```

Add celery.py to your Django project root:

```
# your_project/celery.py

import os
```

```
from celery import Celery

os.environ.setdefault('DJANGO_SETTINGS_MODULE',
'your_project.settings')
app = Celery('your_project')
app.config_from_object('django.conf:settings',
namespace='CELERY')
app.autodiscover_tasks()
```

Update __init__.py to load it:

```
# your_project/__init__.py

from .celery import app as celery_app
__all__ = ('celery_app',)
```

Configure the broker in your settings:

```
CELERY_BROKER_URL = 'redis://localhost:6379/0'
```

Create your first task:

```
# tasks/tasks.py

from celery import shared_task

@shared_task
def send_email(user_id):
    # pretend this is a real email
    print(f"Sending email to user {user_id}")
```

Now from your view:

```
send_email.delay(user.id)
```

That call returns immediately. Celery puts it in a Redis-backed queue and a worker processes it in the background.

Start your worker with:

```
celery -A your_project worker --loglevel=info
```

This keeps your API responsive, even when doing heavy operations. Celery can also handle retries, failures, task scheduling, and result storage.

You can scale Celery workers independently from your web app to meet demand.

Microservices

As your API grows, some parts may evolve faster than others. You may need different scaling strategies, or different languages, or simply want to enforce clean boundaries between features. That's where microservices come in.

Microservices are independently deployable services that communicate via APIs, queues, or other contracts. Instead of one large monolith, you have multiple smaller systems working together.

You might break up your app like this:

auth-service: Handles registration, login, password reset, JWT issuing

billing-service: Handles payments, subscriptions, invoices

task-service: Handles all CRUD and workflow for tasks

notification-service: Sends emails, push notifications, SMS

Each has its own database, its own versioned API, and possibly its own CI/CD pipeline.

In Django, this transition starts by:

Isolating apps with clear responsibilities

Moving toward decoupled APIs (using Django REST or FastAPI)

Extracting services one by one when you need independent scalability or deployment cycles

Don't start with microservices too early. They add operational overhead—network complexity, service discovery, monitoring, and deployment management. Only split services when the boundaries are clear and the benefits outweigh the cost.

Communication Between Services

Microservices often talk to each other via HTTP (using APIs) or asynchronous messaging (via Redis or RabbitMQ). Celery makes it easy to send messages across services:

In service-a, you might enqueue a task:

```
send_invoice_notification.delay(invoice_id)
```

That task can live in service-b, if configured with the right broker and task import paths.

For APIs, tools like httpx, JWT authentication, and OpenAPI contracts help maintain clarity between teams and services.

Be deliberate with communication—avoid tight coupling or calling services in request/response chains that create cascading latency.

These aren't strategies you must adopt all at once. You apply them incrementally as your API matures and your operational needs become more demanding.

By understanding where each tool fits—and how to use it properly—you're well equipped to keep your API fast, maintainable, and scalable, even as usage and complexity increase.

Conclusion

You started this journey by setting up your development environment and writing your first Django REST API endpoint. You explored what APIs are, why they matter, and how Django REST Framework allows you to build them with clarity, structure, and precision. And over the course of this book, you've taken that basic starting point and turned it into a fully-fledged, production-ready backend platform.

By now, you've developed the practical skills and architectural understanding to design clean APIs, implement real-world workflows, and confidently ship secure, scalable, and maintainable backends using Django and DRF. You've gone from defining serializers and handling authentication, to building reusable views, writing tests, and deploying your project with best practices in mind.

But more importantly, you've built more than a backend. You've created a system that behaves predictably, performs reliably, documents itself, and can evolve over time without collapsing under its own weight. Whether you're building internal tools for a company, a public API for third-party developers, or a backend to power a frontend app on the web or mobile—what you now know is enough to build it right.

You've learned to version APIs without breaking clients. You've added Swagger and ReDoc for instant, interactive documentation. You've automated your testing and deployments with GitHub Actions, configured PostgreSQL and Docker for real-world infrastructure, and applied caching, query optimization, and indexing to keep everything fast under load. You've even taken your first steps toward async views, background workers with Celery, and designing a system that could grow into microservices when the time is right.

There's a reason this book didn't rely on abstract metaphors or oversimplified examples. Because building APIs in the real world requires clarity, not cleverness. It requires you to understand why something is done a certain way—not just how to do it. That clarity and depth are what you've built page by page.

Where you go from here is up to you.

You might start by building more endpoints. Or maybe you'll refactor your permission system to better match business rules. You might scale your project across multiple environments, introduce rate limiting, or add observability with metrics and logs. And in time, you may find yourself leading API design across a team or a company—bringing the same care and standards you've now learned to a larger engineering practice.

What matters is that you now have a strong foundation. Not just in Django REST Framework, but in the mindset and discipline it takes to build APIs that last.

Thank you for reading. Thank you for building. Keep writing good code, keep asking clear questions, and always build with the future in mind.

You're no longer just a developer using Django—you're an API engineer capable of shipping software that works, scales, and supports real users in production.

Now go build something meaningful.

www.ingramcontent.com/pod-product-compliance
Lightning Source LLC
LaVergne TN
LVHW080114070326
832902LV00015B/2579